The Hot Flashes

The Hot Flashes

Award-Winning Senior Tap Dance Troupe

Leona Claire Fuller

ISBN-10:0989839222
ISBN-13:978-0-9898392-2-8

Published by the Gluepot Press in Salem, Oregon
editor@gluepotpress.com

DEDICATION

Dedicated to the memory of Jean Johnson, whose vision made the Hot Flashes a reality, and to Bernie Shrum, her loyal sidekick, who helped make her dream come true.

CONTENTS

ACKNOWLEDGMENTS

Paul Richards, my ardent supporter and admirer through all my years of dancing

A huge thank-you to:

My perceptive editors, Macy Hays and Linda Lindholm

My proof-reader's extremely sharp eye, Judy Gilbertson

My consultant, Bernie Shrum, who provided material and photos

Also, much appreciation to:

Jane Hammond, for donating her late husband's poem and tidbits of interest

Barbara Jones, Judy Siegling, Mary Wells and Janice Struve for needed photos

Pat Homan who gave me additional humorous stories to include in the book

Jill Fuller, who contributed two fine poems

CHAPTER ONE
FIRST INTRODUCTION TO THE HOT FLASHES

"Take life by the hand and dance"

Figure 1 The author in costume in San Francisco

"Join the Hot Flashes and change your life." Those words were still ringing in my ears from a call I made to Jean Johnson, owner and director of the senior tap-dancing group "The Hot Flashes."

Will that really change my life?

Widowed for a couple of years and still interested in the stage either as an actress or a dancer, I thought taking dance classes and performing with a senior women's dance troupe might be just the right fit for me.

The previous year was spent at Sue's Dance Studio brushing up on my tap dancing. I had not tapped danced since I was a child in San Jose, California. Actually, my dancing 'career' began in San Francisco at the age of three when my mother took me for ballet, acrobat and hula dancing lessons. Several years later, after a break from dancing, and at a time when money was scarce in our family, my mother somehow scraped together the $1.25 weekly fee for dance lessons at Mrs. Andrucetti's dance studio. Mrs. Andrucetti, a charming lady dressed in long flowing gowns when teaching, introduced me to tap. So, from the age of eight, I was fully sold on that art form. To this day, when I hear music from my first tap dance, "Darktown Strutters Ball", my feet cannot resist shuffling to the first steps of that dance. Music and tap dancing are embedded in my soul.

Sue's instruction, mostly for children, contrasted with the Hot Flashes' single focus on women over 50 years of age. I definitely qualified chronologically on that point. It was time for me to move on from refresher lessons to the challenges of performing.

"Sue, I've learned much from my year with you, but now I would like to try The Hot Flashes. If I'm not satisfied, I'll be back."

Sue smiled slightly, but I could tell by the doubtful look on her face that she didn't think I would be back.

When I phoned Jean about classes available at her studio, she informed me she was starting a new class at five o'clock on Thursdays to accommodate working women. There was one other woman in that category that would be joining me.

Fine. I can handle that.

As I approached the studio that Thursday evening, I nervously looked up at the signs on the tall building in front of me. It read "On Broadway Studio" and "Home of The Hot Flashes." This was certainly not <u>THE</u> famous New York Broadway, but it was aptly named for the location on Broadway Avenue in Tucson, Arizona.

I timidly opened the door and slowly climbed the stairs, clutching the rail with a sweaty palm, all the while asking myself whether I had made a wise decision to leave the familiar instructions and setting at Sue's. At the top of the stairs, I could hear tapping, music, and ladies chattering.

What's all that noise? It sounds like lots of feet. I thought there was to be only one other woman.

I almost turned around to escape down the stairs, but at that moment, a small gray-haired woman appeared.

"I'm Jean Johnson. You must be the person who called about the evening class."

"Yes, I'm Claire Fuller. It sounds like quite a few tappers in there. I thought there was going to be just one other woman."

"Oh, they're from the day classes, but their tuition covers all classes offered. These enthusiastic dancers and performers aren't about to miss out on a single class, day or night."

I peeked through the glass barrier that divided the dance floor from the office rooms. On the floor about fifteen ladies were dancing to the music of "The St. Louis Blues." The choreographer, a slim middle-aged man with a dark receding hairline, frantically attempted to organize the women in various formations as they tapped to this march.

The instructor, whom I later learned was Neal, beckoned to me to jump in anywhere.

Jump in? I have no idea what they're doing. I'm ready to go back to Sue's where I'm comfortable with what I already know.

Before I knew what was happening, I was pulled into line. The dancer behind gently guided me as I attempted to follow the one in front of me.

Oh, I'm so confused. Sue, you'll see me soon. I didn't expect to be thrown into the middle of a dance. I'd anticipated being taught one step at a time from the beginning.

However, the other dancers were kind and patient with me. One woman offered to help me at her home. Another invited me to her garage where four ladies met every Monday morning for practice. I gladly accepted all their help. As time passed, I learned the dances and became a part of the troupe. Memories and the fear-driven desire to return to the safety of Sue's Dance Studio faded.

Little did I know how much my life would really change. Hundreds of performances, beautiful costumes and numerous parades were all to be in my future. I had become enamored with "The Hot Flashes."

CHAPTER TWO
CREATION OF THE HOT FLASHES

"Hold on to your dream. Don't ever give up."

Jean Johnson had a dream to create and direct a senior women's tap dance troupe. However, fulfillment of that dream would not happen for thirteen years. She was living in Pittsburgh, Pennsylvania in 1978, recently divorced, teaching in an elementary school and ready for a change.

One very cold, dreary day, Jean was speaking with her close friend, Bernie Schrum, who had rented a room in Jean's home.

"Damn it, Bernie, I'm sick and tired of this miserable weather. I've had it up to here with teaching, and I'm ready to move. My parents have both died, so there's nothing to keep me here. I want to escape this freezing twenty-degree weather and find a place where it's warm."

Bernie eagerly found a map to explore possible places to relocate. They agreed on Arizona. Together they moved to a state that boasted mild winters and hot, but dry, summers. A friend of Jean's recommended the city of Tucson. They bought a house and became residents, not just snowbirds. They no longer had to fight snow and ice. Jean was finally warm.

To support themselves during those first years, Jean found a job at the Arizona Historical Museum, working in the archives. Bernie hired on at the local telephone company. Both later worked for and retired from the IBM Company. Jean decided to take an early retirement stock buy-out.

Jean was exhilarated. "Ah, now I can sleep late, work in the yard, and no more nine-to-five job." That feeling of freedom soon wore off. Jean started looking for a way to use her talents. Bernie played golf for her fulfillment, but Jean was not sports minded. She was not content to be relegated to Bingo, babysitting and the proverbial rocking chair. She felt that each age should have different enlivening opportunities and challenges.

Jean remembered how she really enjoyed tap dancing as a child, and was good at it, too. She went in search of a tap group of mature ladies that she could join. Jean checked the phone directory, searched local papers, and called senior centers. But she could not locate a group like that anywhere in Tucson, so she reluctantly opted to join a tap class of young people. Her class was composed of mostly seniors all right – eighteen year old seniors in high school! She felt completely out of place there and because of her age she couldn't keep up with their fast pace. However, Jean did meet another mature woman, Gloria Lee, in that class of energetic teens.

"Gloria, remember when I called the Armory Park Senior Center looking for a mature women's dance group? They told me about a lady who gave private lessons."

"Really, Jean? Let's give it a try. Anything's better than tripping over our feet in the midst of a bunch of kids."

They made up their minds to head in a different direction, so they signed up that very day for private lessons with the instructor and choreographer at the senior center.

"Ladies," their instructor announced several months later, "there's going to be a dance competition up in Sedona. Since you both have mastered a couple of dances, why don't you give that contest a try?"

Jean and Gloria jumped at the chance. At last, an opportunity to show off their newly acquired dancing skills. They took the four-hour drive to Sedona in separate cars; their instructor and a friend in one vehicle, Jean, Gloria and Bernie in another. The competition was set to take place at Sedona's local high school. At first, Jean and Gloria were pleased that their instructor would be with them, but she ended up causing an embarrassing, unforgettable situation for her two students.

Jean and Gloria arrived far in advance of the scheduled hour to begin, giving them extra time to relieve their nervousness. While waiting back stage, their instructor appeared in a bright red hat, wearing her skirt wrong side out and obviously inebriated.

"Hey, girls, I've decided you need me to dance with you."

Jean and Gloria were horrified! This lady could hardly stand, much less dance.

"No, no, you're not in any condition to dance. We'll take you back to your motel."

"Oh, no you won't. Get your hands away from me."

The determined woman pushed them away and staggered onto the empty stage. She sat down on the floor, watching the people who bustled about setting up for the competition. Jean and Gloria ran to the stage and managed to pull the poor drunken woman up and half dragged her behind the curtain. They walked her to her car, where she promptly climbed in and locked the doors. She stayed there for hours, missing the entire competition. Jean and Gloria felt both anger and pity toward the instructor, but they needed to hurry back inside to perform the dances she taught them.

It was time for these two aspiring dancers to take their turn in the contest. Dressed in tuxedo-type costumes with top hats, they were ready for their first number. But, horror of horrors, the music, which had not been cued, started before they could get on stage. That threw them off completely on their dance steps.

They didn't do much better with their second number and, at the closing of the dance, Gloria looked at Jean. "What the hell are we doing here?" They broke out in raucous laughter, as they realized they were not quite ready to compete with experienced dancers.

Of course, they didn't win any awards, but they learned two lessons: always wear stockings under their fishnets to not expose bare legs and make certain the music cassette tapes are cued.

Private lessons were not the solution to Jean's visions of using her many talents. She ended her connection with the dance instructor and came up with a new idea.

"Bernie, I've been thinking. There's not a single performing tap dance group for senior ladies in the entire city. Why don't I start a group? I could teach the ladies the basics. Then later I could find a choreographer to take them farther and prepare them for performing in front of an audience."

Bernie looked skeptical.

"You're fifty-seven years old. Are you sure you have the energy to tackle such a big project? You have no experience operating a dance business. You'd need a studio, need to advertise. Most of all you'd need money. Lots of it."

Once Jean made up her mind to make her vision of a senior ladies dance troupe realized, she wasn't about to allow minor obstacles to interfere. She knew she would find a way.

Jean took action. She remembered the former Rockette she met at the Sedona competition. She was a talented lady who directed the successful performing group from Phoenix, winning most of the awards at the competition. Jean decided that she needed to study with her.

"Bernie, take care of the home front. I'm moving to Phoenix for a while."

Jean rented an apartment in Phoenix and spent many hours taking tap dance lessons with the Rockette instructor's group. She studied choreography and learned how to organize a senior tap group from that very accomplished director.

About a month later, Jean arrived back in Tucson armed with a large binder full of notes which she often used as a reference for the next thirteen years. She was ready and eager to take on a new career and establish a dance troupe for women aged fifty and above. Her goals were to teach new skills, which included the art of tap, the necessity of teamwork and the techniques of performance.

"Bernie, how shall I get the word out? I don't want to spend money on advertising when I don't even have a studio or a choreographer."

"Why not take one of our bedrooms and make it into a temporary studio? As for prospective dancers, you know that energetic woman down the street, maybe she'd like to take lessons. She can help you spread the word around, and you can talk it up to your friends."

Jean started by running an ad in a senior paper and received several responses from older women not willing to act their age and eager for a new challenge. Five ladies, all of a certain maturity with stars in their eyes, arrived at Jean's makeshift studio, expecting to be transformed into accomplished tap dancers and to excel enough to perform for others.

With a hint of amazement at their growing numbers, Jean often related to those early days with, "Many of the women came through the door never having danced before but with a dream to do so. Some were widowed, divorced or just bored with the options offered after retirement. But they all had the desire to learn and apply a new skill."

Jean could only take her dancers so far. She drilled them on tap basics and ordered records that provided various levels for beginners from the Al Gilbert Company. Students held onto the bars while a voice on the record gave instructions followed by music. Learning the basics was essential, but the reward was to be using those skills in a dance routine. It was time for the next step.

CHAPTER THREE
THE GROWTH OF THE HOT FLASHES

"A challenge can be the herald of something better to come"

"Ladies, we need a choreographer," Jean announced. "I've taught you the basics and you've learned the steps from the dances Gloria and I performed at the competition, but we're at a point where we need more help."

One of the ladies shouted out, "Jean, I know of a studio in town where we can get some additional lessons. It's called Sue's Dance Studio." So Jean and her students enrolled at Sue's studio. That is the same studio where I was to study two years later. At that time I had no knowledge of Jean and her students.

During the four months Jean's group was at Sue's, they learned one dance which they performed at the annual recital held at a local theater for studio's young students.

Jean's senior ladies' group had grown from five to twenty-two. Discord began to grow between Jean and Sue and also dissension within the group itself. It was time to separate. Thirteen women chose to follow Jean. The other nine formed a competing dance group.

With those first thirteen loyal dancers looking to Jean to take them in a new direction, she had to think of a different approach. Jean needed to find a studio of her own and a choreographer. She knew that commitment would take money. Where would she find the cash? There was only one place she could think of, her retirement fund from IBM. That's what she did to further the vision of her dance group.

Jean rented a dance studio on 12th Street in Tucson. After some searching, she found a gifted choreographer by the name of Neal Cowhey. Neal had an extensive portfolio. Born in Enfield, Connecticut, he took advantage of New York opportunities, studying jazz and tap dancing with acclaimed instructors. In the 1970s he performed with Martha Raye in "Wildcat." Neal choreographed numerous productions and had stage roles in a variety of musicals over the years in Tucson.

Figure 2 Neal & Joel - our choreographers

When Jean met Neal, he was at a low point in his life and reluctant to the task of teaching and preparing a group of mature women to perform.

"I don't know, Jean, it's been awhile since I had on my tap shoes. I'm really not up to it."

"Neal, I think you'd be perfect for my group. I've taken them as far as I'm able. I need your expertise. Besides, being around this group of feisty ladies, I'll bet they'll lift your spirits, too."

Neal took the choreography job with the newly formed group and never regretted it. Jean was right. He now felt a sense of purpose and of use again.

The ladies loved him even though he could be a task master, expecting perfection. He requested each dancer to demonstrate a certain step while he knelt and put his ear to the floor to make certain each was done correctly. He likened dancers to instruments that a choreographer plays. He knew that practice was the means of attaining the perfection desired.

Neal told tales of how he was treated as a boy learning to dance in New York City. The teacher struck a cane on his legs if he did not perform the steps precisely. Neal was never that strict and often enjoyed many laughs with his students.

Jean needed a name for her dancing ladies if she was ever to market the group.

"Bernie, we need a catchy name. But everything I come up with doesn't strike me right. I thought about the 'Dancing Dollies' but I don't like that. Let me think. How about the 'Terrific Tappers'?"

"Oh, Jean, that's a possibility."

"Bernie, I'd like something to fit in with our age group, like 'Hot Flashes'. Nah, I don't think that would work, either."

"What do you mean, Jean? I like that title. Use The Hot Flashes."

"Hmm, let me think. That would spark people's attention and maybe get a few laughs. Makes our dancers sound full of life and not like some old ladies out there barely kicking their legs around. I think that's it! Now I've got to come up with a logo."

At breakfast the next morning, Jean tried various designs on a napkin until she finally arrived at the perfect logo to fit the name of the "Hot Flashes."

It was a headless dancing figure with lightning bolts for the body, arms and legs. One hand held a cane and wore tap shoes on its feet, with a black top hat over the figure. Even the letters "The Hot Flashes" looked electrified.

Jean took her pattern to a shop that specialized in tee shirts and had the logo transferred onto the front of hot pink shirts and some black tees. Pink and black became the theme colors for the dancers. They eventually wore them, with white pants in the summer and black pants in the winter, whenever they went to performances. The Hot Flashes turned a number of heads entering theaters, hotels, trailer parks and senior centers on their way toward the dressing rooms.

The name and logo were registered with the State of Arizona and Library of Congress.

With the logo and color scheme settled, Jean turned her attention to other matters. It became a tribute to Jean's capabilities to locate and keep women committed to the mastery of dance and successfully handling the pressures of performing before an audience.

Building their confidence, Jean inspired the ladies by telling them, "There are thirteen of you, so thirteen will be our lucky number. No one person will be a star. You all are stars." There was an energy, a vital life force, a quickening that passed through them into action. The dancers were waking up each morning excited about their next practice session at the dance studio.

Member Hilda Darland told how, growing up in a family of six children, tap lessons were out of the question. The nearest tap teacher to her home back then was twenty miles away. She put on her first pair of tap shoes at age fifty-nine and was amazed at how Hot Flashes changed her life. Bringing the group together had given ladies like Hilda a second chance.

Jean's responsibilities as director were to modify and polish the dances that the choreographer taught and to prepare the dancers for performances. She also selected and ordered costumes from dance catalogs.

For their first costume, she chose one which made every dancer look good, regardless of size and bulges. The costume consisted of four pieces; a short silver fringe skirt, a silver fringe top that covered a pink leotard for daytime performances and a black leotard for evening, and a stylish sequin-covered hat with pink or black scarves which wound around the hat and hung down behind the head.

As the group grew, these costumes made quite an impression when dancers entered the stage or came through the audience kicking their legs high to

Figure 3 Exiting from "Darktown Strutter's Ball" in our basic costume

the music of "New York, New York." Dancers also reach their audiences through the eye, using color and costuming to create an illusion, like the magician.

The Hot Flashes' early performances were mostly at nursing homes, but they were beginning to make their little group known. However, the dance troupe's limited repertoire hindered them from staging a full show. Once at a senior center, they presented two dances and thanked the audience for their attention. Some folks in the audience were not satisfied.

"We want more!" they chanted.

"That's all we know," Jean responded through the microphone. "Two dances."

"Do them again," they yelled.

So the Hot Flashes gave them what they wanted and repeated those two dances.

As the months moved along, Neal taught the ladies several new tap routines, enough to present a half-hour show. That did not mean the dances always ran smoothly. For instance, Jane, one of the dancers, concentrating on her steps to "Lullaby of Broadway", inadvertently moved her sparkly cane too close to her hat, which caused it to adhere to the hat. There the cane hung from her hat until she finished the dance. She never lived that down.

During another dance, Eileen, who knew how to add humor into an embarrassing situation, felt her fringe skirt falling down. She picked it up and flung it into the audience to much laughter, while continuing to dance in her pink leotard. The show must go on.

About a year after the Hot Flashes group started, more ladies joined the original thirteen dancers until it had grown to at least twenty-five performers, enough to make an impressive showing in Tucson's annual Copper Bowl Parade. For practice, Jean took the dancers out on a quiet side street and drilled them in marching and dancing techniques.

Jean stressed, "We want to do everything we can to impress the judges and win an award."

The day of the parade, the ladies were decked out in their pink and silver costumes and grouped together in their assigned spaces. Bernie walked beside them, pushing and sometimes pulling a golf cart loaded with a boom box blasting out music. These mature high steppers in their marching boots strutted along with smiles to light up the world.

Two ladies, carried the new Hot Flashes banner and led the way, followed by a very proud Neal decked out in a black suit. He signaled directions to the dancers behind him. When they reached the judges' stand, they stopped and performed their dance routine, hoping to achieve a high score.

Later, at a nearby park, the parade participants gathered for the award ceremony. How thrilled and surprised the ladies were when they heard the judges' announcement. "The 'Most Inspirational' award goes to the Hot Flashes." It was the high point of their day.

At home that evening, Bernie started the conversation, "Jean, the Hot Flashes are becoming recognized as a special group. More women will be joining us. Wouldn't it be nice to have our own studio?"

"You better believe it, Bernie. I am so dissatisfied with the 12th Street studio. It's in a very seedy part of town and the dancers are concerned about attending evening classes."

The owner, a dance teacher of young children, charged Jean $200 a month rent, and Jean had to schedule her classes to fit in with his schedule.

"You know, Bernie, my dream is to find a studio where I could be solely in charge of its operation and a place where we could provide dance classes for mature adults only. We really need a place of our own."

Jean's wish was about to come true.

.

CHAPTER FOUR
THEIR OWN STUDIO

"So start out today with faith in your heart and climb till your dream comes true." Helen Steiner Rice

When one door closes, another one opens. On September 13, 1993, Jean found what was to become the open door at 7036 Broadway, at Kolb and Broadway in Tucson. The man who owned the building was willing to lease the upstairs which served as a dance studio ten years previously. All the bars and mirrors had been removed, so Jean and Bernie could see the work and expense ahead of them. Before they signed a lease, Jean asked a favor of the landlord.

"We need a private entrance to the studio so the dance students don't have to traipse through your part of the building. Is that a possibility?"

The owner, taken aback about such a request, looked thoughtful and answered, "Let me think about it. I'll see what I can do."

Shortly thereafter, a new private door was built just for the dance studio. Through that door many women entered as prospective dancers and exited as precision performers. Jean's door had literally and figuratively opened.

Having a studio with a private entrance was no small achievement. However, one look at the condition of the interior of the studio might have discouraged most dance teachers from signing a lease, but not Jean. With her vision and Bernie's handy skills, they saw beyond fallen roof partitions and plaster on the rough wooden floor. At their own expense, they transformed that studio by installing mirrors and bars, hanging shades on the tall windows, and refinishing the floors. A coat of white paint brightened the large room. Windows ran the length of the studio and the mirrors on the opposite side seemed to visually double the area. Some of the dancers donated furniture for the main office, Jean's office, the video viewing room and the coffee room.

Imagine the first day the studio was ready. The eager dancers running up the stairs, slipping on their tap shoes and tap-tap-tapping onto the floor ready to learn what Neal might have in store for them in their very own studio. Broadway was an inspirational address, even in Tucson, Arizona.

Finally, Jean had her own sunny studio, a dependable choreographer and an expanding group of enthusiastic dancers. Jean was providing a new horizon for senior women. They were given new challenges, new skills to learn, fun ways to exercise, new friends and an opportunity to serve by performing for the community. Knowledge about the Hot Flashes was spreading around Tucson. People soon recognized that they were a first class professional dance team.

Practices and rehearsals were held at least three times a week. Most of the ladies wore tee shirts, trunks or shorts, and dance tights during classes and practices. Jean participated in the lessons so she could learn the routines well enough to polish or modify them later and also to be able to perform with the group.

Jean's vision did not stop there. She dreamed of the Hot Flashes becoming world-renowned precision dancers, performing for hundreds of audiences beyond the Tucson limits, dancing in New York, earning gold medals in competition and performing on cruise ships.

Jean stressed that commitment, teamwork, willingness to learn dance routines, personal performance and helping others were essential attitudes and behavior for performance excellence and positive group function. Behavior that exhibited lack of team spirit, inability to dance, excessive self-concern, no cooperation or personal responsibility would be grounds for a resignation request.

She liked to tell us, "I will not be the director of a ragtag old girls' group, but I am proud to be the director of the first-class Hot Flashes women."

When I joined, there were two groups; the core group who had been with Jean from the beginning, and the intermediate group who entered later and learned a few dances separate from the core group. I was first placed in the intermediate group.

Jean set up strict etiquette guidelines for classes at the studio. "Ladies, there's to be no gum chewing, either here or during performances, and please do not wear perfume or cologne. Only water bottles are permitted on the dance floor, and definitely no food. Kindly do not tap or talk when the instructor or director is speaking, as a couple of you are doing right now." She gave those two ladies a steely-eyed glance.

Rules for performances were even longer:

1. Dancers are to wear false eyelashes, heavy makeup, applying ample blush and bright red lipstick. No blue eye shadow.
2. No earrings. Dancers are to look uniform.
3. Dancers are required to wear ultra-shimmery light toast tights.
4. Glasses are not to be worn.
5. No talking on the stage, and no one is to tell another how to dance or what to do concerning dancing. Dancers are to pay attention to their own dancing, and bossing others will not be permitted.
6. Keep your hair neat. No long hair hanging down around your face.
7. We are considered to be on stage as soon as we arrive at the place where we are performing and representing the Hot Flashes.

Jean enforced the rules and managed the business end as if she were still running IBM.

As they say, rules are made to be broken, and those of us who broke them got an earful from Jean. She was a tough task master, but that was her way of keeping control and presenting a top-rated group. Several women did walk out through the years or were asked to leave. They learned that if dancing were any less strict and strenuous, it would be called football.

Some felt they were only there to have fun, but it was not all fun. The dancers spent hours and hours in classes, in home practices and in rehearsals, repeating again and again specific movements till everyone made the group look like a precision team. The dancer Martha Graham used to say that the freedom to dance means discipline. That is what technique and practice are for—liberation. Those who were dedicated to reaching that goal hung in there and stayed loyal to Jean, even through difficult times.

All those Hot Flashes rules and regulations were in force when I first nervously climbed those Broadway studio stairs in the fall of 1993. My new, adventurous dancing career was set to begin.

.

CHAPTER FIVE
ADJUSTING TO THE DANCE ROUTINES

"One must have chaos within oneself in order to give birth to a dancing star." Friedrich Nietzsche

"Join the Hot Flashes and change your life." Jean Johnson's words still echoed through my head when I returned for my first paid lesson.

I don't like this uncomfortable feeling of being the new kid in the dance class. I'm confident I can learn the dances, but are those dancers going to accept me? After all, they've been with Jean a couple of years and performed at a number of venues. Well, I showed up, I signed in, and I paid the $25 for the month, which covers one lesson a week, so I'm going to get out on the floor and do my best.

Actually, at that first lesson I did more observing than dancing as I watched the dancers review the routines they already knew. Their dancing seemed to be a natural extension of the music. To say I was overwhelmed would be an understatement. Yet, I was drawn to a talented group of ladies who, like me, had always wanted to dance. It would mean hours and hours of practice to reach their level.

One very kind dancer reassured me, "Neal won't have time during this hour to teach you those dances, but you're welcome to come to my house where I have a practice floor and a tape recorder. I'll help you catch up." That kind offer was music to my ears.

The first dance she taught me was "Alley Cat", a very simple dance which I learned in a couple of weeks. That was followed by "Chattanooga Choo Choo" and "Little Brown Jug" which were more complicated and took me much longer to master. It takes time to get a dance right, to create something memorable.

I lived in a small one-bedroom apartment and my only practice floor was in the tiny kitchen. Fearing to scratch the floor with my taps, I practiced in sneakers and at least mastered the sequence of steps if not the correct flaps and shuffles.

Another dancer invited me to join her and four or five others at her home each Monday morning at 7:30, where we practiced on a large wooden floor in her garage. Occasionally, neighbors strolling by were drawn by the music and the tapping sounds and stopped to watch us.

During classes I participated in the new "St. Louis Blues" dance they were learning that first night I visited the studio. The Arizona State Fair was opening soon and Jean planned to have both groups of the Hot Flashes begin with that number. The best part was that I was permitted to debut in that dance. It was my first opportunity to put on my tap shoes, draw a deep breath and dance with those incredible women.

The day we were scheduled to perform at the Arizona State Fair in Phoenix, I was up at dawn to apply my stage makeup and to make my first attempt to attach those tricky false eyelashes. What a job to spread the glue and place them on correctly just above my natural lashes. Sometimes I placed them too high or too low, too far to the right or too far left. Good thing I got up at 5:00 a.m.

It took a half-hour drive in the early morning traffic to catch a ride with another dancer and her husband, then another two-hour ride from Tucson to Phoenix. We were due to perform at noon on an outdoor stage. Our dressing room was outside behind the stage, but we were hidden from view by screens that had been set up. It did not take long to dress for our first number, as we donned blue and white striped coats, blue trunks, silver tap shoes and tall sparkly blue band hats. Some of the ladies attached their lashes there, but not me. Mine had been on for hours, and that's where they stayed for the rest of the day. Besides, I had more important concerns.

Oh, please, don't let me mess up my first performance with the Hot Flashes.

We lined up, ready to go on for that first dance. Bernie started the music as the Hot Flashes high-stepped onto the stage to the "St. Louis Blues March." I do not recall making any mistakes in this rather complicated dance of various formations. When it was over, I hurried off stage to help others change into their basic costumes which they wore throughout the

Figure 4 The author entering for her first performance with the Hot Flashes

hour show. After changing into my street clothes, I settled down in the audience to watch the rest of the show, and longed for the day I would know all the dances.

Bernie took videos of all the shows, and it was customary for her to present a free copy to a new dancer's first performance. So the proof is in the video that I did well, but it may have been beginner's luck.

At a later performance of the same dance at the Moose Club one evening, I really caused some problems. The stage was at an angle to the audience and I, confused, turned backward when everyone else faced forward. I was so embarrassed. Once a mistake on stage is done, it is done. That tormented me the rest of the evening. When the dancers went for a snack after the show, I packed my costumes and escaped to the isolation of my home rather than face the others.

Jean required that all dancers view the video of the previous performance the next time they were in the studio. "You are to check your own mistakes so you can correct them."

With dread, I watched the videos with Jean, for fear she might catch the mistakes I made. Even with poor eyesight, she possessed an eagle-eye, both at the performances and with the videos. Woe to you if your hat was on wrong. If Jean detected my mistakes, she didn't mention it. Perhaps the camera was focused on another dancer. "Betty, your hat was way back on your head. How many times have I told you? Hats are to be placed down firmly on the forehead."

Jean was also a stickler about keeping our lines straight. Time and time again, she scolded us for uneven lines by reminding us backstage after performances or at the studio. It was so easy to get caught up in the dance itself by concentrating on our steps that we forgot to use our peripheral vision to check our position with the dancer beside us. Sometimes, I was guilty of being ahead of my line.

Dancing may appear easy, delightful and glamorous, but the way to precision and achievement is no easier than any other great task. There are times of confusion, frustration and disappointment, those small deaths during a performance.

During those first few months with the Hot Flashes, I worked as a substitute teacher. I also was a grocery store demonstrator, giving out food and drink samples, with a sporadic work schedule. As a result, I participated mostly in evening performances.

One afternoon when I was free, I applied makeup and eyelashes, packed my two costumes and headed off in ample time for a 2:00 p.m. performance at the Odd Fellows Hall in Tucson. Searching up and down streets for the address I had been given, I found nothing that resembled such a building. I stopped at a corner market for directions. Workers there had never heard of an Odd Fellows Hall in that neighborhood. Then I saw a church with many cars in the parking lot.

Perhaps they could help me locate the Odd Fellows Hall.

Entering the lobby, I looked around for some welcoming person, but nobody was there. Voices were coming from what I thought was the sanctuary, but I was too timid to interrupt what possibly was a special service. Totally dejected, I turned around and left, went home, removed the makeup and unpacked my costumes.

I learned later that the venue had been changed to that very church where I had stopped. Jean didn't realize that I had not been notified about the change. Well, that disappointing day, I didn't find the Odd Fellows Hall, but found that I was the odd fellow out, out of the show, that is.

The year 1994 brought many requests for Hot Flashes performances, an average of six per month. Jean once told me that she never had to call an organization to schedule a show. Groups noticed her ad in the yellow pages and phoned the studio. Our performance fees were reasonable at $50 to $75 for a half-hour performance.

Shows were held at retirement centers, mobile home parks, the county fair, hotels, the Oktoberfest, senior centers and private clubs, anywhere there was a staging area and a dressing room. Checking carefully on the addresses and location of the performances, I managed to make it to these places without getting lost.

Being a member of the Hot Flashes had its advantages. Returning to the stage to dance was one of the most rewarding and wonderful things I had ever done for myself. Meeting new people, learning new skills, teamwork and techniques of performance were not the only benefits. I now knew in my heart that an older woman like myself could still be proud, vibrant, respected and productive. I soon discovered for myself that a Hot Flash could also find love for the second time.

CHAPTER SIX
FINDING LOVE A SECOND TIME

"Autumn is just as nice as Spring ... Never too late to fall in love."

Little did I know as I applied my makeup and those pesky eyelashes that April day in 1994 that I was about to indirectly meet my future husband.

We were booked to perform at the Aztec Inn following the monthly Widows and Widowers luncheon. Wearing our basic string costume with a pink leotard, I appeared twice with others in my group performing "Alley Cat" and "Chattanooga Choo Choo," but I could not do "Little Brown Jug" with the other dancers because I had not been cleared by Jean for that dance.

Okay, I'll just dance to the music on the carpet backstage.

After the show I changed into street clothes and went among the crowd to sit with my friend, Billie, who had come to watch our Hot Flashes show. A man was playing keyboard so members of the Widow and Widowers club could dance. While glancing at the couples on the dance floor, I noticed a tall, slim, handsome fellow dancing with the president of the club.

She's so lucky to be asked by him to dance.

"Billie, why don't we sign up for next month's luncheon? It looks like an interesting group," I suggested.

She said, "Sounds good to me."

The following month, after the luncheon, Billie and I were heading for the parking lot when the same tall fellow I had noticed previously came along beside us.

"Will you be attending the Italian-American luncheon?" he asked.

"Oh, yes, we both bought those tickets the keyboard player was selling."

"I'll see you there, then." And he rushed on ahead.

"I think he's interested in you," Billie observed.

If anything, he's interested in Billie. She's so much prettier than I am.

At the Italian-American Club, I noticed that same gentleman had come in after us and found seating at a faraway table.

What a long afternoon that was!

We expected to eat at 1:00 p.m. Instead, we were forced to sit through two hours of an organ recital put on by the keyboard player's novice organ students before we could finally line up for our spaghetti feed.

In the line, I was finally able to converse briefly with that man whom Billie thought was attracted to me. After we exchanged names, we learned we had one thing, at least, in common.

"Paul, do you drive a silver Nissan? Last month when I was driving home from the luncheon, I passed who I thought was you in that model car."

"You got it right, Claire. Why are you asking me that?"

"Because I have a silver Nissan, too."

Now I really got his attention.

The conversation ended there as we quickly turned to fill our plates and hurry to our seats to appease our hunger at this late hour.

Billie and I almost did not attend the next luncheon held in May. We had just returned from a tour to northern Arizona and both of us were too exhausted to consider another event just two days later. However, there was a message on Billie's answering machine from Pat, the president of the group, begging us to attend. It was the last meeting until the fall and she was expecting a small turnout. So, to please Pat, we showed up.

Paul arrived shortly after we did and asked if he could sit at our large round table, already occupied by several ladies. However, they soon became a blur as Paul and I focused only on each other discussing what we had in common – our cars. He advised me on how to change a headlight if the need arose. Thank goodness, I was never faced with that problem. Not a truly romantic conversation, but I found everything he had to say was fascinating.

I also learned he was leaving soon to spend the summer in Oregon before returning to Tucson.

"I'll be camping my way through the national parks, and I plan to return in late August."

Lunch was served, we listened to a guest lecturer from Legal Aid, and then the music began. Paul asked me to dance, but it was more like swaying back and forth in one place as we talked, and talked, and talked. When the music stopped, he handed me a postcard with his Tucson address on it.

"If you're interested in getting together again, send me a response."

Later, as he walked past me, he chuckled, "Remember, the postman only rings twice."

I like his sense of humor, but now I have to decide if I want to return his card.

For two days I hesitated before dropping that postcard and a letter in the post office box. Widowed for four years, I was uncertain whether to become involved in a new relationship. I suddenly knew that there was a reason we met. I had more to experience and more to learn in this lifetime. Maybe this was crazy, but I would rather be crazy and happy than alone and sad.

The postman did not ring even once at Paul's residence. That is, it was ten days later when I received a call from him. He had just found that letter in his mailbox.

What? It took ten days for a letter to go a couple of miles across Tucson!?

We met several times before Paul planned to leave on his summer journey. I sent him off with a huge batch of homemade cookies to keep him satisfied and thinking of me throughout his trip.

One has to try every little trick to catch that dream man.

Paul returned at the end of the summer. He courted me until the following May, when we were married in the lovely recreation room at my apartment complex. All the Hot Flashes were invited to witness the ceremony.

So that is how the Hot Flashes helped me find my second true love.

Whether that dance performance at the Aztec Inn was the cause, or whether my decision to attend the Widow and Widower luncheons brought us together, I prefer to think I first caught his eye while I was tap dancing. When I asked Paul his opinion, he responded, "It was fate that brought us together to live happily ever after."

Paul became a great supporter of my dancing and the Hot Flashes. He rarely missed a performance. He stood at the back of the room during the entire show, warming up the audience or awakening those who nodded off as he shouted out "Yea", "Right on", and "All right." His enthusiastic prompting probably led to the many standing ovations we received. The dancers loved his encouragement. He also helped Bernie, who was in charge of the music, by giving her thumbs up or down to regulate the volume.

What a great life companion I had found!

Paul drove me to my performances, carried my costumes, never tired of watching the same dances over and over. He always claimed he did not notice any of my mistakes which I related to him in full as we drove home. It was comforting to know he was in the audience at our many shows or as an observer during parades.

As a child, I always wanted my mother at my stage performances to gain her approval. Now I had the man I loved to give me much needed support. How proud I was to be a part of the Hot Flashes, and how proud I was to have a man like Paul as my number one fan.

CHAPTER SEVEN
HAZARDS, PARADES AND A WORKSHOP

"We should consider every day lost on which we have not danced at least once." Friedrich Nietzsche

Some events stay in your mind forever. One unforgettable incident occurred at the Sunsites Resort in Pierce, Arizona.

The Hot Flashes dancers were all suited up in our string costumes and waiting in line to enter the room where we were to perform. One of the ladies turned to Jane who was next in line, and in a low, shaky voice whispered, "That floor looks awfully slippery. I think I might fall."

"Don't say that, Dee," Jane exclaimed.

The music to "New York, New York" began just then, and out we went, kicking high. Just as I entered the room, I heard the audience let out a collective "Ohhhh!" as Dee slipped and fell onto that hard floor. She had injured her wrist. Her prediction had come true. Someone helped her over to a chair and wrapped a blanket around her shaking body.

Earlier, Bernie had spread rosin on that asphalt tile floor to reduce the danger of the dancers slipping, but it obviously was not sufficient. The performance had to continue, but it was a harrowing night for all the dancers. We attempted to execute our correct steps while minimizing our movements to keep from falling, all the while feeling concern for Dee. We tried to remind ourselves that 'dancers don't fall, they just make level changes.'

One of the husbands drove Dee the ninety miles back to Tucson. At the emergency hospital, X-rays showed that her wrist was shattered in several places. It took many months of treatment and several surgeries before recovery. That incident ended Dee's dancing days

Tap dancing has its hazards, especially for older women with fragile bones. In addition to having nimble feet, strong arms and wrists are required, plus a good sense of balance. Dancing is strenuous, arduous activity that that takes training that rivals the Olympic athletes. In the studio, we applied strong taps while dancing and moved freely without concern of falling. The routines become possible, but never easy or safe.

Conditions were different each place we performed. Many of the floors were slippery, especially those made of asphalt tile. That night at Pierce was not the first nor last occasion that a dancer would fall. Through the years, I often recalled Dee's fall as a reminder to focus and keep control of my feet.

My first full year with the Hot Flashes was an exciting time for me. Not only did I gain experience performing for all types of organizations like the women's clubs, military reunions, retirement homes, church groups, and state and county fairs, but I progressed enough to be in my first parade as a tap dancer. When I lived in Washington State, I had square danced on a moving flatbed truck, but to tap dance through the streets of Tucson with crowds cheering me on, I could think of nothing more thrilling.

For days prior to the Copper Bowl Parade in Tucson, Jean marched us through neighborhood streets with Bernie walking beside us playing the music from her boom box.

Jean hollered, "Watch your spacing. Line three is creeping up on line two.

You're not keeping your lines straight as you turn the corner. Let's do it again. Look to the center." She drilled us until we were finally ready for the big day.

I awoke the Saturday morning of the parade tired and achy all over with symptoms of a cold or the flu. Determined to be in that parade, I donned my costume, applied the makeup and of course those irksome eyelashes, and headed downtown to line up for the parade. The Hot Flashes had been assigned space number fifty-seven. We stood for an hour shivering in the December Tucson weather.

Once the parade began, being fifty-seven of ninety participants, it took fifteen minutes before we began to move. Two ladies carried our large, pink and white Hot Flashes banner, with Jean next behind the banner leading us.

We walked several blocks until we began to pass spectators. Then Jean gave us a hand signal to begin our dance routine. Besides rough pavement, we had to avoid old flattened train tracks and dodge droppings from the horses ahead of us, while smiling and waving at the people we passed. Keeping an eye on Jean, we followed her directions of dancing, marching, and then dancing again.

When the parade ended, we felt a sense of exhilaration and accomplishment. I had completely forgotten about my pending illness. However, when I got home, I took to my bed and stayed for the next few days, nursing that cold. Each day, under the covers, I relived that wonderful parade and looked forward to the next event. I found dance to be one of my most basic and relevant forms of expression.

On occasion, Jean set up dance workshops with other talented instructors who offered different styles of dance from those we were learning from our own teacher and choreographer.

One of these was a man named John who was in town for a brief period before heading back to Chicago. John came bustling into the studio on a Monday morning, full of energy and ready to teach us the complicated steps to "Back in Business" from the musical show "Dick Tracy." First, John divided us into four small groups. The first group began a short routine, then the second group joined in, followed by the next two groups, until all were dancing together. The music had a challenging rhythm which added to the difficulty.

John returned three more Mondays to work on that dance. And he added another, easier dance to our repertoire.

"You'll like this one. It goes to "Boogie Woogie Bugle Boy.""

What a relief! Something familiar.

We learned that dance in two sessions. For years, we opened our shows with that rousing "Boogie Woogie" number. But "Back in Business" caused problems for us. Sometimes dancers would be absent from one or more or the groups, which threw the dance off balance. John returned about two years later for a drop-in visit at the studio to see how we had progressed.

"John, I'm sorry to tell you," confessed Jean, "that we no longer perform "Back in Business. However, "Boogie Woogie" has become a staple for us.

Come on, gang, let's show him that dance."

By the smile on his face, we could tell that John was well-pleased with our demonstration and preservation of at least one of the dances he taught us.

My wish to be in another parade came true just three months after the Copper Bowl parade, when we Hot Flashes signed up to participate in Tucson's St. Patrick's Day parade. Decked out in green leotards under our basic string costumes, it was fun being in the midst of those red-wigged leprechauns who were riding on floats or decorated trucks. By March, Tucson is warming up, so, by the time we had marched and danced a few blocks, perspiration was dribbling down our faces.

Oh, I hope my eyelashes don't fall off. We must not touch our faces. It's not professional. Just keep smiling and waving at the spectators cheering us on.

When the parade ended, there was a euphoric feeling of accomplishment, but it was a bit of a letdown, too. I was thrilled to perform in a parade to show that senior dancers are capable and have the energy to dance and march for two miles or more. We loved showing people the laughter, fun and joy of dance. I didn't want it to end, but there would be other parades.

As the months passed and people learned more about the Hot Flashes, bookings increased. We were gaining more experience at places such as the Ramada Inn, Elks Club, Pima County Fair, Holidome, Gaslight Theater, Viscount Hotel, The Forum, Rincon Mobile Home Park, Doubletree Hotel, Oktoberfest and many more. All we required was an uncarpeted 16 by 24-foot stage or floor and a nearby dressing room, large enough to accommodate our growing number of performers.

Soon it was time again for the State Fair. This time, I applied the eyelashes with confidence.

How excited I am that I qualified to perform.

One very sweet and soft spoken woman, Nila, had joined the Hot Flashes four months earlier. Hers had been a hard-scrabble life. She lived alone near her elderly parents and made a small salary as a nursing home aide. Always wanting to dance, somehow she scraped together enough money to pay for the city bus ride to the studio and for one lesson per week.

Nila learned only one dance well enough to perform. It was Herb Alpert's "Whipped Cream." For that dance, Jean ordered by catalog a gorgeous Latin costume of purple, green and yellow ruffles with a feathered headpiece to match. Whenever we appeared on stage in that colorful costume, we could hear the audience murmuring "Beautiful" and "Awesome!" Nila managed to pay for that costume, perhaps with help from her parents.

On the day of the fair, Nila's son drove her from Tucson to the State Fair. On the lineup, "Whipped Cream" was scheduled toward the end of the hour. That mattered little to Nila. As soon as she arrived, she donned her costume and waited back stage while the other dancers rushed in and out, changing costumes. Nila sat patiently, always smiling, never complaining, and waiting for her one grand moment to appear on stage.

After her dance, Nila beamed her widest smile. She was ecstatic, and made the rest of us proud of her one dance performance. She must have really loved dancing to stick to it against all odds. It gave her nothing back but that single fleeting moment when she felt alive on stage. She changed back to street clothes and departed immediately with her son back to Tucson.

Nila left the group a few months later for financial and health reasons. Others may have thought of her as a poor soul, but I shall remember her as a woman who set a goal and with determination achieved it. Although she learned only one dance and owned just one costume; that was her fulfillment.

The Hot Flashes presented opportunities for any woman fifty and over. Nila came to us with her particular dream. Many more would join us, each with her own dream. For those with persistence, their dreams of dancing as a living art and more came true.

CHAPTER EIGHT
FIRST COMPETITION

"Courageous women with a lot of style." Tina Naughton, *KOLD-TV*

Bernie stuck her head through the dressing room door. "Showtime in five minutes."

Jean called out, "Let's line up for 'New York', short to tall. Remember, I want those kicks thigh-high. Will you women over there stop practicing your dance steps? If you don't know them by now, you never will. Quiet down and let's center. I want you to focus on what you'll be doing."

While waiting in line, I prayed I would not make any glaring errors, especially where the video camera would catch them. Helen, the dancer just ahead of me in line, connected her little finger with mine for good luck. We continued to do this at every performance.

Jean moved us out into the hallway and closer to the entry. Bernie started the music as Jean led us through the audience to the stage area. We formed a semi-circle, stood in our Hot Flash pose, each dancer standing slightly turned, feet beveled and hands flexed, with big smiles.

When we were all on stage, the music stopped. Jean grabbed a microphone, walked to the center of the stage and shouted out, "We are the award-winning Hot Flashes." Applause and usually some laughter came when she said that. "We are not over the hill but on our way to the top."

"I'd like to introduce the women. Will all of you dancers in your fifties step

Figure 5 Jean in top coat and hat - sometimes worn as emcee

forward." Those in that age group stepped out from the line and waved. This was repeated for those in their sixties and seventies. Anyone over eighty received a special introduction. Ruth St. Denis appropriately said that when you are sixty and still dancing you become something of a curiosity. If you hit seventy and can still get a foot off the ground you're phenomenal to the public.

"You're probably wondering my age. Well, I was born before the war, and the North was winning."

My husband, Paul, had made up that joke and Jean used it forever after. Jean, then introduced the first dance, ran back to the core group and performed with them while we intermediates left the stage.

After the dance, Jean breathlessly ran back to the microphone to introduce the intermediate's dance as the core group left the stage to prepare for their next number. Between dances, Jean informed the audience of the location of our studio, invited interested women to join us, and reported on the number of classes each week.

On occasion, the show was held up because of a costume change glitz in the dressing room. Jean covered our delays well because she was adept at ad-libbing witty lines to fill the time. She was fond of stating, "The Rockettes change costumes in a minute and a-half, but the Hot Flashes require three!"

Back in the dressing room after the show, Jean frequently commented on the successes or failures of our performances. "Claire, you were out in front of the others again. All of you were late getting out on stage. I can ad-lib only so long. Other than that, it was a good show." There were to be many successful uneventful performances, but also many with numerous mishaps and unexpected situations.

On a Senior Day at the Pima County Fair, while dancing on the outdoor concrete stage, strong gusts of wind blew the hats off a couple of dancers. Bernie retrieved them and handed them back to the hatless performers. They placed the hats on their heads and never missed a step. During the dances that followed, strings on our costumes waved in the wind like hula skirts. We were surrounded by music, dancing and joy.

After that show, Jean fell ill. She collapsed on a chair, dizzy from very low blood pressure, and waited there until paramedics arrived and revived her. It certainly frightened us all out of our wits and we felt helpless. After that incident, Jean often said, "If anything like that happens on stage, just dance right over me."

Another time, we presented a one-hour show for the Lions Club. Before the show, Jean told us, "We might cut some of the dances because there are a lot of elderly in the audience. They may get tired."

Dancer Eileen, who had just turned seventy, could not refrain from asking, "How old is elderly?" We all laughed. Jean kept the show at its scheduled one-hour length.

A couple of embarrassing situations occurred at the Savoy Opera House one night. First, Sally, on stage, punched her hand into one of the pillars during her dance. Luckily, it was not a serious injury, and she kept right on dancing.

The other incident happened at the start of our "Whipped Cream" dance. Our audience of retired officers had been drinking several hours before we arrived and had become rowdy. We were dressed in Latin ruffled costumes and as the music began we moved forward to the audience, opening and closing our skirts as part of the routine. Those men let out a rowdy whoop and raised their hands in surprise.

My gosh! I didn't expect that! I feel like a cheap chorus girl.

We finished the dance, but I vowed I would never again perform in that costume so close to the audience, even if it meant breaking my line.

Whenever there was a request for a performance, Jean or Bernie always informed the caller we were tap dancers in need of a proper venue. However, when we arrived at the Cascades Retirement Home, we were presented with three options: dance on the carpeted stage, perform at the salad bar behind pillars, or perform on the tiled floor below the stage. We chose the third option. Thank goodness, it was only a half-hour show. We never went back there.

June 21, 1995 was a memorable day. The Hot Flashes had been invited to perform at Hi Corbett Field as entertainment for the Toros' baseball game. As people filled the bleachers prior to the game, we danced on the grass below. Yes, we tapped on grass. While performing the dances "One" and "Sophisticated Swing", a worker on a machine smoothed the field. That raised dust all over us. But, we performed those dances to near perfection in spite of stumbling in the rough grass and wearing those hot tuxedo coats in the ninety-degree temperature. We had redeemed ourselves from last year's fiasco on that very same field.

Previously, the dance we presented required multiple changes of lines and formations. A few of the dancers became confused, so instead of the dance concluding with flair, it had ended as a tangled mess. Jean, who was observing us from the bleachers, told us later, "You all looked like a can of worms." She continued to remind us of that disastrous day, using that same expression, even after that near-flawless performance a year later.

During half-time on that same June day in 1995, we danced to "42nd Street" in one long line on the rough walkway of the bleachers. The most striking memory I have of that night was to see the Hot Flashes name in big letters flashing on and off on the scoreboard. We were so proud!

The next month on July 4, the Hot Flashes were booked at The Forum, a retirement home. Appropriate for the day, we opened the show with a new number, "Stars and Stripes Forever." Dressed for the occasion, we wore red, white and blue jackets and blue band hats with white feathered plumes. White gloves and silver shoes completed our outfits. We marched, tapped, changed formations and, near the end of the dance, Jean marched in from the back of the stage, carrying the American flag. Folks in the audience, some with tears in their eyes, rose to their feet at the sight of the flag. At future performances, that dance became our standard grand finale.

On a heat-record-breaking day that same month, the Hot Flashes were invited to perform at a private home as entertainment for a Gay Nineties birthday party to honor guests ninety years or older. We dressed in two bedrooms and filed through the kitchen to perform on the shaded five-foot deep patio, instead of the sixteen-foot stage we usually required. An audience of eight viewers sat in the shade and bravely endured the hot weather conditions. The hostess had arranged for a television camera man to record our program. We began the show with the dance called "One", wearing our heavy white tuxes and top hats. What a challenge as we dodged posts and each other in the narrow space. Some of our tall hats rammed the eaves above, making loud clunks as they fell off our heads. Pebbles caught under our taps and destabilized our balance. Undaunted, we moved through the other dances as though we had a full stage.

Our hostess, Helen, was forever distracting the audience by shouting out and talking with others as we danced. During our show, she pushed herself into the front line next to me and attempted to dance with us. Poor Carolyn, in the second line behind us, was completely hidden.

When the music stopped, Helen turned to Jean, "Could you interrupt the show for a brief interview with one of our gentlemen here?"

Jean, who never permitted intermissions for our shows, responded on our behalf, "We only have two more numbers and the women are hot and tired." She then signaled to Bernie to start the music, and we continued. We never made the television news but that pleased Jean. The crowded area did not show us at our best. Helen's interruptions and comments spoiled what could have been an interesting feature story about how the Hot Flashes braved the 112 degree heat to dance for a group of seniors in their nineties.

When the Hot Flashes were just getting started, they performed in nursing homes for little or no pay to gain experience. Later, as the group became known throughout Tucson, we stopped taking bookings from nursing homes. However, when Jean received a call from Valley Health Care with a plea for us to return for a third time, she could not refuse their request.

So, off we went to perform on their large, but extremely slippery floor. The residents were seated all around us, so we alternated our dances in different directions in order to give the audience a fuller view of the dancers.

As we posed, waiting to begin, an impatient lady behind us called out, "Hurry up. What are we waiting for? Let's get on with it." She was probably tired of looking at our backsides. In addition, throughout the show, another woman critic yelled out insults. "That's not right. That's not right. Get the hell out of here. You've already done too many."

As we were leaving the floor for the last time, the critic offered one more comment. "Now that you've made fools of yourselves, you're leaving." Perhaps she had been a dance teacher in her younger days. Most of us found her amusing. We did not let it bother us, but presented our best in spite of a few distractions. Our music and the dances no doubt brought back heart-warming memories to most of the residents in the audience.

One disaster after another occurred at the Marana Fair, located just north of Tucson. The outdoor stage was too small and carpeted, so we resorted to dancing on the tennis court in the hot sun. The audience was sparse and some of them talked or ignored us.

There was no microphone for Jean and no speakers were provided since we had not been assigned to the main performance area. Tables were set up for us on the court for our cases. We hung our costumes on the chain link fence.

Between dances, Carolyn whispered to me, "It's taking me a while to get my motor going."

I nodded, "Mine, too, except my motor keeps starting and stopping, especially when one of my lashes fell down over my left eye." I had discreetly removed it and kept dancing as a one-eyelash dancer.

The next incident was worse. During the dance "One", Sally neglected to remove her chin strap. As she raised her hat, the strap slapped her in the face, breaking the strap completely. Of course, she kept dancing and smiling while ignoring her stinging cheek. In another dance, our cowgirl hats were so large that they slid from side to side when we sharply turned our heads. Mine slipped down and partially covered my eyes.

There were more mix-ups, including when one of the helpers took my fringe skirt to Jean. We wore each other's skirts during "Boogie Woogie." Good thing we were close in size and height. As it is so often, the greater part of our misery or happiness depends on our positive attitudes and not our unfortunate circumstances.

The next performance at the Quality Inn Suites, before a bomb squadron reunion, made up for the previous fiascos. Before 300 people, we truly shined as professionals. After the show, we heard comments such as these:

"I have a complaint. Why wasn't this show longer? I could have gone on watching the show forever."

"Please come to Philadelphia. I'll pay your way. That is, if I win the lottery."

A lady from Phoenix said, "You're better than any of the groups in Phoenix."

At the Doubletree Hotel, I forgot my fishnet stockings which we wore over our regular tights for one of our jazz numbers. Jean's rule: "If anyone forgets an accessory, no one will wear it." She was strict about uniformity. So, we all danced without our fishnets, which diminished the effect.

I felt terrible.

From then on, I made a list of all my costumes and the accessories for each and checked the list carefully as I packed for each performance. I rarely forgot anything after that.

One morning at the studio, Jean asked, "Anyone here interested in performing at the "I Love Dance" competition?" About eight arms shot up, including mine.

Oh, boy. A new experience.

We met at the Quality Inn Suites on a Sunday afternoon, the first dance competition for most of us. Gathering in one of the motel rooms Jean had rented, we changed into our "Boogie Woogie Bugle Boy" costumes, covered them with shirts and skirts and sat in the audience for a couple of hours watching very talented youngsters compete.

At last, it was our turn to show them what we could do. In our forty-plus category, we were up against only two other dance groups. Before we began the dance, Jean warned us to start far back, to move up with our first steps to the brighter area and to look and smile at the three judges.

When the music started for "Boogie Woogie," I fumbled those beginning steps, due to my nervousness with the extremely slippery floor and to my worry over moving up close enough to the judges. After we were successfully in place, I noticed the middle judge smiling and seeming to enjoy our performance.

Maybe she'll vote for us.

For our second number, we rushed back stage to change into our "Sting" costumes that we had previously piled in a corner of that crowded dressing room. Back on stage, we performed "The Sting." That seemed to go well, except I was off the beat on the first triple-time step.

Much to our surprise, the Hot Flashes were given a second-place trophy for

"The Sting" and a first-place trophy for "Boogie Woogie." That qualified us to compete in either New York or Lake Tahoe competitions.

We were thrilled and to cheer our success we celebrated with snacks and drinks in Jean's motel room, proud to have earned those beautiful trophies.

Figure 6 Bernie and Jean proud of the trophies we earned at the "I Love Dance" competition

We chose not to go to either of the advanced contests in Tahoe or New York since we would have to finance our own trip, plus fees to participate. Competitions are not free.

Our last performance of 1995 was the Copper Bowl Parade in December. It was perfect parade weather, sunny and sixty-eight degrees. We missed Jean's presence and leadership, but she was not ready to perform that day due to the recent loss of her son.

Bernie handled the parade preparations very well. She lined us up in the proper order and told us when to start moving. Bernie no longer had to pull a golf cart containing the sound equipment. Instead, now and for future parades, Carolyn and Charlie generously offered their van. Bernie perched in a chair atop the van and played the music on the recorder beside her. However, during a test before parade time, the battery caused the sound to be distorted. They solved that problem by connecting the recorder to the cigarette lighter. The music then came through loud and clear, enhanced by speakers on either side of Bernie.

Figure 7 Bernie atop Charlie & Carolyn's van before the Copper Bowl parade

Numerous spectators lined the streets as we marched and danced to a Spanish tune. My dedicated husband Paul followed us as we moved along. A special treat for me was that my daughter, son-in-law and two granddaughters from Eastern Washington watched from the bleachers near the end of the parade. What a lesson to them that one does not just have to live the length of their life, but can live the width of it too.

Afterward, while we gathered in the parking lot, Carolyn poured cups of cold, refreshing Gatorade. How good that tasted to us warm and weary parade dancers!

That was my sixth parade and my third in the Copper Bowl. What a wonderful way to end the year with a total of forty-five performances and parades in 1995.

Jean had taken the Hot Flashes a long way from the humble beginnings in a room of her house. We now had an attractive studio of our own and capable choreographers. The studio schedulers regularly received multiple requests for the award-winning senior tap dancers, the Hot Flashes.

If we thought 1995 was a great year, what could we expect in 1996? Jean, with her visionary ability, was about to bring us new and exciting experiences

CHAPTER NINE
ALL-AMERICAN CRUISE COMPETITION

"Inspirational! They tap their way into our hearts inspiring all of us to do more." Phyllis Ehlinger, *KSAZ Radio*

Five, six, seven, eight… tap. If you were to walk into the Hot Flashes' dance studio Monday through Thursday morning, Jean or Neil would be calling this basic instruction, preparing the dancers to begin on the first beat.

The Hot Flashes had grown to about sixty members, so changes had to be made. The core and intermediate groups joined to become Group One. Less experienced dancers were part of Groups Two and Three, and beginners were placed in the fourth group.

I gave up my part-time jobs and focused on the Hot Flashes, committing three days a week to lessons, practice at the studio and participating in every show.

As rental fees increased, tuition rose in proportion, until we dutifully paid $85 per month plus a $5 fee into a fund which Jean used for flyers, business cards, and accessories for the dancers. All the dancers were quite willing to pay the price, anything to promote their Hot Flashes.

Figure 8 Group 1 - Ready to perform in their "I've Got Rhythm" costume

Figure 9 Group 2 - Taking a bath during the "Splish Splash" dance

Figure 10 Group 3 - Posing for the number "Tango"

Figure 11 Group 4 - Dancing to the "Grand Slam Charleston"

We began the New Year with a bang on a three-day cruise from Los Angeles to Ensenada, Mexico. Our group was not along just for the ride, but to compete in "The All American Dance Championship." Tap dance groups from Arizona and California also took part. In addition to paying for the cruise, we had to pay $7 per dance to the competition organizers. Being in eight dances really added up expenses for me.

The first morning, I met with others dancers to check out the stage, review our spacing, and to psych ourselves up for the afternoon competition. Later, I returned there alone to retrieve a program I had left behind.

Looking at that huge smooth stage, I envisioned myself executing every step perfectly while standing tall and smiling at the audience. As I returned to my cabin to gather my costumes and apply my makeup, I looked forward to joining my fellow dancers on that stage and giving it all we had.

Backstage, our so-called dressing rooms were more like tiny closets. Riva, a performer who was only in one dance, stayed back stage to help us with quick costume changes. For me and others, she was a miracle worker and a godsend.

When the competition ended, I was exhausted from performing in eight dances, plus all those costume changes and the climb up and down steps between selections. But, I felt elated and pleased. I had made only a few errors, in spite of a sore throat, a headache and an achy body. I was ready to go home.

Wait! We had one more day on the ship, and there were awards to be presented by the three judges. We cheered and clapped our hands each time for the two gold and eight silver medals the Hot Flashes received. Much to our dismay, the groups from the Phoenix area were given most of the gold medals.

A woman at one of our past performances told us, "You Hot Flashes are better than any of those groups in Phoenix." The judges here certainly didn't agree with her assessment. However, "Special Awards" were given to the Hot Flashes for "Smiling Faces," "Precision," and the "Swinging Sisters."

Winning the final presentation, the "June Taylor Award," made us especially proud, because June Taylor was a famous choreographer known for her large precision dance group. Our faces beamed! Additionally, the judges kept detailed critique notes on each of our dance performances, which they gave to Jean. She used these suggestions to help us perfect our presentations for future competitions.

During this competition, another much younger group from California in the lineup before us, had danced to the music of "Boogie Woogie Bugle Boy", wearing identical costumes as ours.

I wonder how our seemingly copycat costumes will go over with the judges.

When we finished our number, that competing group, still in their costumes, gave us a standing ovation from the balcony.

What great sports they are. I feel like a star.

Upon our flight back from Los Angeles, we were greeted at the Tucson airport by a photographer from Channel 4. He filmed our dance troupe filing through the airport in our bright Hot Flashes tee shirts. It was played on the 6 p.m. news and on the next day's morning news with a report on all those medals we had won.

No sooner did we return from the cruise competition than it was time to prepare for the Tucson Senior Olympic Festival held also in January. Hundreds of viewers were sitting on the bleachers when we arrived that morning at eight. Our dressing room was in one section of the closed snack bar. We hung our costumes on large food containers. When they opened the snack bar for business, we were partially exposed, but luckily dressed in costume.

By the raised outdoor stage, we stood shivering in the cold in spite of the sun, and welcomed the signal to climb up on the bumpy stage to open the ceremony with three dance numbers. In the stands, each cheering section sported particular colors and had its own cheerleaders. The enthusiasm among those youthful seniors was a pleasure to see, as we danced through our numbers of "One," "American Patrol," and "Stars and Stripes." The spirit of that morning carried forward with the Hot Flashes as they met new challenges.

Occasionally, our bookings did not work out as anticipated, but we had to do whatever it took, as Bernie often reminded us. One case in point was the Indiana Club. For the first time, this was an engagement we could not complete. We were scheduled to be at the Sirloin Stockade at 1:00 p.m. for a half-hour show. The spokesperson for the Indiana group greeted us at the entrance.

"You can all dress in our restroom. And I'll show you where you are to perform." She led us to their small partitioned dining room.

"But that's on carpet. We're tap dancers," Jean responded, "there's no way we can do this."

Jean then spoke to the club members and explained why we could not put on a show for them. Bernie turned the music on for "New York, New York. That day, we did 'whatever it took' as we turned and kicked our way out of the room.

What a letdown!

However, we did not always decline a carpeted stage. One evening we arrived at the Viscount Hotel to learn the disappointing news that the raised stage was carpeted.

"No one told me you needed an uncarpeted stage," the lady in charge said, as she directed a few choice swear words at Jean.

This time we did dance on the carpet, but it was not completely soundless. edThat stage reverberated to the pounding of our feet, a terrible racket. In spite of a shaky start, the audience seemed to love us, and that angry lady who had greeted us led a standing ovation at the end of our show.

A group like the Hot Flashes, to be successful, required organization and cooperation. Jean took charge of dancers, choreographers, and costumes, while Bernie assisted with music, bookings, sound equipment, and studio repairs. They both relied on volunteer help from dancers.

Jean appointed a very capable woman, Bobi Brown, to do the lineup list of dances to be performed at each show and to be in charge of the costume room. I was asked to assist Bobi with costumes, and we spent many an hour organizing and reorganizing in that little costume room. Woe to anyone who entered that room without our permission.

I also helped in the office answering the phone, writing thank-you notes, and taking bookings. My tasks included posting future performances in the sign-up book and writing them on the board in the hallway.

Hilda, the treasurer, kept a record of the financial report of tuition fees and Hot Flash dues. Just about everyone pitched in to help in one way or another, but Jean had the final say in all aspects of the business.

To assist her with the four groups, Jean chose captains for each dance team. The duties of the captains were to lead the dancers during their practices and to help with backstage preparation.

Barbara Jones, a skilled tap dancer, was the captain of my group. She caught on quickly to the new steps that instructors taught us. Because we did not wish to go home to practice the lessons incorrectly, we rushed to Barb as soon as the teacher departed and pleaded, "Will you review the new steps for us?" She was always happy to help us, patiently going over the new routine as many times as we requested. If I could practice new steps as soon as I returned home, then they usually stayed in my memory.

Before I married Paul, I practiced on a 4 by 4 foot board in my bedroom. Luckily, the apartment below was rarely rented out, so my tap noise bothered no one. After our wedding, Paul and I moved to another apartment building. I continued to use that same wooden practice board in the bedroom until it began to splinter.

One day we purchased a new board, but it would not fit into the trunk of the car. Paul solved the problem. "I'll carry it through the streets while you drive the car home."

As I drove the several long blocks home in the light rain, I passed Paul setting the board down to rest, then taking up the board again, as he fought the wind blowing against him. He made it home successfully. Anything to support my dancing practice. I so appreciated his sacrifices and help.

As dedicated as I was to regular practice and never missing a lesson, I could occasionally foul up a perfectly good dance. It happened at the Rincon Country East Trailer Park one morning before 250 people during our dance "Heaven Hop."

Figure 12 Innocent nun sisters in "Heaven Hop"

For that dance, we wore long black habits, black and white head coverings ordered from a costume catalog. During the last part of the dance, we raised our skirts just to the knee to display our red garters. This always elicited a laugh.

So far, so good for me. And then the worst happened. Oh, good grief, the veil is slipping down over my face. What shall I do? Just keep dancing.

At last, the entire veil fell down around my neck. The audience roared with laughter. As I humbly left the stage, I could hear Jean's comment to the audience, "One of our sisters has been de-veiled."

Figure 13 My headpiece has become a veil

I made certain I was never de-veiled again. Rather than tying it on, some kind person sewed elastic into the covering and made it fit snugly around my head. Speaking of sewing, that skill was never my forte. If the subject was ever mentioned, I felt fear forming in my eyes. I did minor sewing tasks when forced, but preferred to pay accomplished seamstresses in our group or an alterations worker in a tailor shop to make necessary costume modifications.

Jane, who was also sewing-challenged, and I announced to our fellow-dancers, "We are the co-chairs of the Non-Sewing Club. If you want something sewn, don't bring it to us. Instead, we'll bring ours to you." The women laughed. After that, when any sewing was required, they would tease us by saying, "Let Jane and Claire do it."

Dressing rooms at performances were often disappointing. Once, the dancers were assigned a storage room that had wires hanging down and puddles of water on the floor. Somehow, we avoided being electrocuted. Another time, we were given a small shed lined with bales of straw. We were forever brushing off bits of straw from those costumes. But, sometimes a dressing room worked to our advantage. That happened at the Tucson Community Center.

When the Hot Flashes arrived and entered the building, we found a small carpeted stage and two tiny dressing rooms awaiting us. Jean moved us into the ladies' restroom instead, a less than desirable arrangement. However, I had my own private dressing room in the handicap stall. I lay my garment bag on the floor and hung costumes on door hooks. What more could I ask for?

From the small unusable carpeted stage, Jean changed the performing area to a tiled entry room. Our taps sounded loud and clear. Most people stood to watch us, since there were few benches.

The community center master of ceremonies introduced us in grand style, but caused a distraction when he began to clap to the music and off the beat, too. At the end of the show, as we stood in our Hot Flashes pose, he gave us a brief acknowledgement, then immediately stole our thunder by giving greater attention to someone's black puppy. We waved to the audience and kicked off.

Two days later, we were at the Pima County Fairgrounds to perform for the Holiday R.V. Club. Eight hundred folks from all over the U.S.A. gathered in one of the buildings to watch our show. Oh, the perils of dancing! The large elevated stage was uneven. I rammed my toe twice on a raised part.

At the back of the stage, the dancers had to avoid stacked bales of hay set up for their western theme. Downstage, we had to be careful not to step on the speakers or fall off the narrow stage. At the conclusion of the show, all 800 people stood to give us a standing ovation. That was our reward, to see hundreds of people looking up at us and applauding.

About ten days later, the Hot Flashes put on a show for the Sigma Phi organization. A head table was set up for eight officials of that group. Throughout the show, those women looked very stern. Back in our dressing room, one of the dancers remarked, "They looked like they could have been judges at the trial of Nuremberg."

There were lots of mix-ups in our dances. Some dancers could not remember their places in "City Lights." During our "Heaven Hop" dance, the sisters drifted around in confusion.

I believe they think they're already in heaven.

Surprisingly, we received a standing ovation from the stern head table.

One of our outstanding shows that year was on March 29, 1996. The Sabbar Temple Shriners hired us to be the entertainment for their annual fundraiser. The previous morning we rehearsed on their carpeted stage, with a promise that they would provide a wooden stage for the night of the performance. According to their word, they laid a large wooden stage on top of carpet by the time we arrived that Friday evening. It was a joy to dance on that surface.

Our dressing room was a long way from the stage, down three steps, through doors located at the back on either side of the stage. We then hurried along a rough, dimly lit walkway to finally reach a large outbuilding. Lots of helpers assisted with quick costume changes so we could make it back in time for the next dance.

That night, a young couple presented several ballroom dances, which gave us a restful break. We later learned this couple's child had a rare disease. The money raised that night was donated to help their ill child.

Such a good feeling to know that we Hot Flashes helped make that financial assistance possible.

The Shriners told us they wanted Hot Flashes shows to be an annual event. Sure enough, they asked us back each year after that.

Sometimes, we did two shows at different times on the same day. One spring day, the first show was scheduled for 10 a.m. at the Pima County Fair. When we arrived an hour earlier, we found puddles of water all over the outdoor stage. With a borrowed broom from the restroom employee and reams of paper towels, Bernie and helpers managed to have the stage dry by performance time.

If only that was the worst of our problems.

The dressing room nearby was locked, and we had to find someone to unlock it. Then, we could not use it, because hornets had taken up residence. So, we just dressed outside in front of everyone. Somehow, we managed to change from our fringe to nun costume and back to the fringe again, out there in the open, and in record time.

Gosh, I hope the audience keep their eyes on the stage. Maybe those folks walking by won't notice us. Gotta keep my mind on what I'm doing.

After the show, men and women crowded around while the dancers were getting out of costumes and told us, "You looked like you were in high school." That wonderful compliment energized us to rush over to our 1 p.m. performance at the Radisson Hotel to dance for the Welcome Wagon organization. No need to hurry, as they kept us waiting in line backstage as they read the longest list of announcements I had ever heard.

Come on. Let's get this over with. We want to dance.

Dance we did, with the happiest smiles we could put forward no matter how tired we were. When the music started, we were ready. Folks often remarked that we looked as though we were having fun. They could forgive our tapping errors, if they even noticed them.

Now that the Hot Flashes were comprised of four groups, we had more time to change costumes between numbers, so were not always in a panic. Problems did occur, though. Someone might need help putting long-sleeved gloves on, to be zipped up, or require assistance with a hat.

Another might frantically search through her case for an accessory item only to realize it was left at home. We remembered Jean's rule, "If one dancer is missing an article, none of the other dancers will wear theirs. You must all look uniform." That included shoes, too, since we all owned gold, silver, black or white shoes that matched certain costumes.

Sometimes, a dancer volunteered to stay out of a number, which, of course, added to the dilemma by having to rearrange positions, prior to rushing out to the stage.

I wonder if the Rockettes had these problems?

One thing for sure, we Hot Flashes never matched the Rockettes ability to change costumes in one-and-a-half minutes. Jean required new Hot Flashes to serve as helpers with costume changes until they were ready to perform, which sometimes took several months. They stayed in the dressing room, ready to assist as we breathlessly dashed back to change into another costume. Those helpers were invaluable.

One of the longest and most tiring days occurred when we were scheduled to perform at the Hilton Hotel for the Knights of Pythias. That morning I was up at 5:00 a.m. to prepare for the sale of used and new costumes and accessories at the studio. We made over $300. I attended a master class conducted by Bryan, a new choreographer, from 9:00 to 11:00 a.m., followed by practice for that night's show.

By 9:00 p.m. when we finally started the show for one hundred people, I was thinking more about turning in for the night than putting what energy remained for dancing and costume changes. Backstage, I put on turquoise gloves for "Favorite Son" instead of white. Then, when I caught my error and changed, I jammed two fingers into one glove finger, pulled them out and had to start over.

Out on stage, I lost my balance on the second step during "Thoroughly Modern Millie," but did not fall. In "Heaven Hop," I had not tied my rope belt properly, which caused only a short piece to hang down by my right hand. When it came time to twirl the rope, there was nothing for me to twirl, except my hand, which moved round and round.

Figure 14 "Thoroughly Modern Millie", the ending that usually earned an applause

We rarely did encores, but because that audience was so appreciatively responsive throughout the show, we presented "Stars and Stripes" as an encore. Getting ready for that number, I was halfway out of the dressing room when I discovered I had forgotten to put on blue trunks under my short jacket and quickly yanked them on.

Oh, that oversight could have been embarrassing!

Then I ran out with only one glove on, but a helper caught that mistake in time, just before I entered the stage. Once on stage, I smiled as though nothing had happened. If any of us made an error while dancing, we better not make a face. We were told the audience would not notice a mistake if we kept moving and smiling. However, whenever it happened, I always felt all eyes on me. It might even be captured by that nasty video camera or, even worse, Jean's eagle eye. Others surely felt the same way.

There were times when the dancers smartly covered their mishaps. For example, while performing at the Forum on the 4th of July, Helen's shoe flew off her foot during "Stars and Stripes," but she nudged it aside with her foot and finished the dance with one shoe. At the same program, Liz fell down during "Piano Roll Blues," but jumped back to her feet, as though nothing had happened, and finished the dance. Real troupers!

Every year the Hot Flashes were invited to perform at the Oktoberfest, a fundraiser for muscular dystrophy, always held in September.

I don't know why it's called Oktoberfest when it's put on in September. I guess it sounds better than "Septemberfest."Looks better in writing, too.

We danced under a large tent on a slippery floor with an uneven surface. The dressing area was outside behind the tent, hidden by a large parked trailer. One mishap for me occurred when a tall red feather fell off the headband that was part of my "Thoroughly Modern Millie" costume. Two helpers, Katie and Faye, taped it on with duct tape just in time for me to dash onstage for that number.

The crowd, composed of all ages, screamed and whistled before and after every dance. During "Millie" they went wild as we stepped forward, shaking our shoulders in a sexy move.

I love the rousing applause, but I think the beer consumption contributes to their exuberance.

The next afternoon, we returned for a repeat performance for another large crowd. They cheered and hollered, causing us to beam with pride.

One more glitch happened to me when a new sequenced belt on my "All That Jazz" jacket fell off shortly before going on. I thought someone had sewed it on, but it was only pinned. One of the helpers pinned it on just before I took my place on stage.

Maybe I shouldn't always be expecting others to sew for me. That's what I get for being the co-chair of the Non-Sewing Club.

After each Oktoberfest performance, Paul and I always stayed to do the Chicken Dance played by a great German polka band. Such fun!

I never get tired of dancing! I can express beauty with no other instrument than my own body. To dance is to live.

Phyllis, owner of the local KSAZ radio station, frequently invited the Hot Flashes to perform at various fairs and home shows. She and Dan, one of her announcers, made all arrangements for setting up stage and sound equipment. Dan always gave us a stirring introduction, building the troupe up as though we had just arrived from Broadway.

During the Senior Fair arranged by Phyllis and Dan at the Kino Athletic Center, we were met with another challenge. We had to dance on plastic placed there to protect the new wooden gym floor. We could now add plastic to our growing list of odd surfaces to tap on. It was actually easier to dance on the smooth plastic than carpet.

Folks at the Senior Fair were standing to watch us. They gave our efforts a wonderful response. I saw some people shaking their heads in apparent amazement.

At the Smugglers Inn, the facility provided a postage stamp-sized floor for us; only 12 x 12 feet. Those in the second line hit their arms on the back wall and in "Millie" our arms hit each other because of close proximity. Our audience, the Retired Republic Airlines Pilots, were very reserved during the show but gave us a standing ovation. Or else they were applauding the flag Jean brought in at the end of "Stars and Stripes".

Let's hope both!

Our group received a $111 tip in addition to the $100 fee we charged. Plus a man from Irvine, California said, "I'll pay all your expenses if you will perform there."

Hope he carries through. I've got my bag packed.

We never heard from him. Promises, promises.

In Jean's Hot Flashes, all mature women were welcome. The only requirement was to be a woman fifty years or older and show a commitment to performance, excellence, and teamwork. At that time, the Hot Flashes ranged in age from fifty-two to eighty-three years old. Once Jean was asked during a television interview the admission qualifications to join the Hot Flashes. Her response, "You have to be ambulatory."

Experienced dancers, women who had never danced in their lives, women of all shapes and sizes, and those with various handicaps were all invited. At various times, women with hip and knee replacements, Parkinson's disease, breast cancer or macular degeneration stayed as long as they were able.

While some dancers were hit with age-related ailments, they were so committed to the success of the Hot Flashes that they danced in spite of their infirmities or returned once they were healed. Something kept calling them back to the stage. Jean, herself, began to cope with serious health problems. That concerned us all.

Without her, what would happen to the group? What a shame to end the dreams of those dedicated dancers. At a time when the Hot Flashes' good name was well-known around town and beyond, when they were almost to the top of that mountain, would they just close up shop, left with only memories and photos to remind them they were once part of the proud Hot Flashes?

CHAPTER TEN
SENIOR NATIONAL OLYMPICS

"Real women don't get hot flashes; they get power surges."

One evening, I received a call from the hospital, a call I did not want to hear. "It's Bernie. Jean's in emergency. She's having difficulty breathing."

I rushed to the hospital. Jean's son, Danny, was just coming out of the emergency room. To my surprise, he told me, "You can go in and visit her."

Standing at the foot of her bed, I talked with Jean for just a few minutes. Although her face was covered with a clear oxygen mask and she was still struggling to breathe, she managed to give me a few directions on how to manage the studio, even throwing in some light humor about her situation.

"Don't I look cute? At our next show, I'll walk out on the stage with this oxygen mask and in my gorgeous hospital gown, and shout 'We are the Hot Flashes.'"

How can she make a joke when she's coping with such a dire experience?

I must admit I laughed at such a scenario. It gave me relief, and I'm sure it helped her. Jean recovered and was back in the studio in about a week, but there were to be many other episodes of that nature that sent her to emergency. Each time we feared for her life.

To add to our concern, on one occasion both Jean and Bernie were hospitalized at the same time for similar breathing problems. They shared a room. But placing them in one room with beds side by side was like putting two lions in the same cage. At home, where each had her own room, Jean could read her books and watch serious dramas on television. Bernie, on the other hand, was an avid sports fan who could sit hour after hour to cheer on every seasonal game that came along.

Besides quarreling over what to view on their one hospital television set, Bernie related this story about when Jean needed to use the bathroom.

"Jean, ring for the nurse to help you."

"No, I can't wait. I'll just pull my IV stand with me. Oh, gosh, why am I having so much trouble? What's wrong with this thing? I'm all tangled up. Damn it! Bernie, come and help me."

"No way, Jean. I'm calling the nurse."

"Never mind. I just yanked out the IV."

"I'm going to ask for another room, as far away from you as I can get," Bernie shouted at Jean.

Nevertheless, whenever those two were together in the studio, they became a comedy team. When one was relating an experience, the other contradicted, and they had all the dancers roaring with laughter. Wherever the two went, they created their own wild stories. In any case, their humor erased our worries about the fate of the Hot Flashes.

They are hilarious. They ought to join up and call themselves Frick and Frack.

One evening, we were scheduled to perform at a place called 11-Mile Corner, seventy miles north of Tucson. It was way out in the boondocks and we spent an extra hour searching in the dark for the 11-Mile Corner. At last, our search came to a successful end when we spotted a huge hangar-like building which sat on a part of the county fairgrounds.

Because both Jean and Bernie were in the hospital that night, I was designated to be the Mistress of Ceremonies and one of the husbands was chosen to play the tape recorder. Unlike Jean, I was not an impromptu speaker who could come up with witty statements, so I came prepared with note cards.

Oh, what I would give for a teleprompter.

I did garner laughter from the audience when I announced, "We're the only group who promotes hot flashes."

The disadvantage in being emcee was I had to stay out of some of the dances because of limited time to change costumes. However, as I stood off to the side and watched the other dancers, a wave of pride came over me. They all looked so beautiful and their precision was perfect. These were not dancers who just wanted to dance, these were dancers who had to dance and make the music visible.

After Jean and Bernie recovered from their hospital bout, they were back to take charge of studio affairs. The Hot Flashes were not going out of business. Jean continued to promote and publicize our dance group, taking advantage of every creative opportunity. New openings were always popping up, and the first of several opportunities for us to climb another rung on the ladder would be occurring in a couple of months.

In the meantime, Jean, who now had to lead a more relaxed life style, stayed out of the performances, but still worked with us to polish dances created by hired choreographers. She ordered costumes from many catalogs stacked high in her office and emceed for our shows, health permitting.

During an interview with the *Northwest Explorer*, a local publication, Jean emphasized, "We're not just a bunch of old ladies tripping the light fantastic. We're a precision dance group patterning our act after the Rockettes." Jean believed in us, and we were determined not to disappoint her.

In May, 1997, one of our big moments arrived. On a Thursday morning, Jean asked, "How many of you would like to participate in the Senior National Olympics to be held this year in Tucson at the University of Arizona stadium?" All hands shot up!

"But here's the catch. I just received the invitation last night, and the opening ceremonies are to be held this Saturday. You will have to report for the first rehearsal at 6:00 p.m. tonight. Now, how many of you can make this commitment?" All thirteen hands rose again.

Those of us who had appointments or engagements for that night and the next two days scurried around to cancel them, so we could report on time for the required rehearsals and performances.

Arriving at the stadium that warm evening, we were greeted by a man and woman who introduced us to the Young Americans, a very talented group of men and women ages 15 to 21 years from California who were to be part of the entertainment. We were heartily welcomed by them and treated with great respect.

Out on the grass, we joined the Young Americans for warm-up exercises. Then, a couple of them led us in routines we were to perform on the field for Saturday night festivities. Robin, a woman from Australia, took charge of us after that and kept us busy the remainder of the evening with various tasks, such as practicing escorting athletes up on the shaky stage. We filled in for the athletes. A lovely full moon gave us the light we needed to learn our movements. We were dismissed at 9:30 p.m. completely exhausted and confused.

I'm trying to remember which arm movements at the correct times during the singing and when to march and when to turn. Oy vey! Why was I so eager to be in the National Olympics?

Next morning at eight o'clock sharp, we were at the studio to practice last night's new routine. With Jean reading the instructions, and Char Walker, one of our quick-study dancers demonstrating, we practiced the movements for a couple of hours. Following the practice, we watched a video that was taken of the previous night's lesson.

With all that stuffed into my head and body, I should know it well by now. Everybody else seems to know what they're doing except me.

By 5:30 that evening we were back at the stadium for a dress rehearsal. We wore our blue band jackets, blue band hats and white flat tap shoes. Of course, we could not tap on the grass, it was just to complete our costume. We practiced for four hours, busy all the time.

I'm seeing some improvement, but I really need three weeks to learn this instead of three days.

A brief rain shower during the rehearsal sent us rushing for shelter under the stadium bleachers. Once the rain stopped we were given a special treat. Some of the Young Americans sang their rendition of "Somewhere over the Rainbow" just as a real rainbow appeared in the sky. So touching and beautifully sung. A choral group in blue robes, who were part of the program, sang their songs, including one of my favorites "God Bless the U.S.A."

Figure 15 Dress rehearsal for National Senior Olympics

At last, Saturday, the day of the festival arrived, and we checked in at 3:00 p.m. for one more rehearsal. Out on the field, we struggled against strong gusts of wind which, at times, literally knocked us off balance.

Group One of the Hot Flashes were asked to do an extra routine called the "star formation." The game plan was for us to run on the field with 6-foot plastic pipes on our shoulders, set them down on the grass in a 5-point formation, crouch down on our knees, making ourselves as small as we could while young teen girls spread out long colored banners. Then, we had to rush off the field.

Will I get this right for tonight?

The rest of the afternoon we rehearsed the previous dance routine we had been taught. Supper was spread out for all entertainers. We gobbled down sandwiches, potato salad, brownies and soda to give us renewed energy for the evening's festivities.

At 6:30 p.m., the "Celebration of Athletes" began. It was time to do our star formation. The Olympics Committee issued white tee shirts labeled with large letters "Senior Volunteer" on the front to wear with our white shorts. When the signal was given we dashed out to do our star. I nearly was crushed from both sides as others rushed on and off the field. Recalling that expression, "be careful what you wish for," I thought back to that morning I eagerly waved my arm to participate in the Senior National Olympics.

The evening was not over yet. All our dancers rushed to the bathroom to change into our band costumes. For security reasons, we were instructed not to leave our belongings in the bathroom, so we piled them into Bernie's car which was unlocked and not secure either. The would-be thieves must have assumed the car was locked and passed it by. As we stood at the side of the stadium, the athletes slowly paraded by us to enter the field. We greeted each group of athletes by state, introducing ourselves and congratulating them on their achievements. I was reminded that it also takes an athlete to dance, but one who additionally is an artist.

Robin led us into the stadium where we sat with the choir and watched the parade of the athletes. What a sight! Each state's participants were uniformly dressed. For example, Arizona athletes proudly showed off purple and white outfits, but New Mexico's was the brightest, sporting burnt orange and dark brown sweat suits.

Toward the last part of the evening, the Hot Flashes' great moment arrived. We filed onto the field, with part of us facing the west bleachers on one side of the stage and the rest looking to the east bleachers. From the tops of the bleachers we must have looked like ants.

How exciting it is to be before such a huge audience! Maybe it's worth it after all.

Perhaps they can, at least, see how our white shoes define our feet in striking contrast to our blue jackets.

The music began, we sang our song and performed our dance movements. It happened quickly and was over with just a blur in my memory. I do remember that it was a grand, warm evening, the winds had died down, and it was a privilege to perform before 25,000 spectators. More importantly, we helped honor those senior athletes who refused to grow old, including ourselves.

From dancing on a cloud at the Senior Olympics, we drifted down into sadness a few weeks later when we learned that Neal Cowhey, our first choreographer, had died. He taught us that good choreography must fuse the ear, eye and mind. He departed the studio a year before, because teaching dance became difficult for him as he coped with serious illness.

The first sentence in a newspaper account of his death stated "Tucson has lost its fiddler on the roof." This was in reference to Neal's past performances in several productions of "Fiddler on the Roof." His lean and lank figure, silhouetted upon a rooftop for the opening number, fit the part perfectly.

At Neal's memorial service, my eyes kept returning to his tap shoes on display with other memorabilia. They took me back to a happier time. The Hot Flashes loved to tease Neal, so for his birthday, five of us decorated a 3-foot high carton as a music box. Since I was the shortest, they chose me to be the ballerina in the box. The day of his birthday, we sneaked the box into the studio. Dressed in a pink tutu, tiara on my head, I crouched down in the box with a recorder. When they brought Neal onto the dance floor, I pushed "start" on the recorder to play "Happy Birthday" while everyone sang. When they reached the "happy birthday dear Neal", I popped up, arms in a circle above my head as I turned myself around in a ballet pose. Neal thrust his arms up in surprise, his mouth open, as he threw himself onto the floor. He laughed till the tears came.

Yes, Neal, "you tapped your way into our hearts" to quote from a poem written to you by the Hot Flashes in 1993. You worked us hard, but you made our classes fun and taught us some terrific dances. We will always remember our special Neal Cowhey.

From the day Neal left us, Jean had to search for replacement choreographers. She found several from the university, but they didn't stay long once they graduated and moved on to advance their dancing careers. However, we were never long without an instructor, including those temporary choreographers.

Figure 16 Performing "Happy Feet" on another day for the National Senior Olympics

In the meantime, requests for our performances kept pouring in. That kept me busy posting dates, times and locations on our bulletin board. One of those requests came from the Tucson Women's Symphony Organization where we were to wrestle with another stage challenge.

Scheduled to immediately follow a Dillard's Department fashion show, we had to use their T-shaped ramp. Not only that, the stage was covered with muslin material, but our taps could be heard. At the rear of the stage, a few of our dancers were forced to perform on bunched-up muslin and to occasionally drive their taps into metal strips under the muslin.

When I looked out at the audience, I saw a sea of faces extending back so far into the shadows, I could only make out a few dim figures. Those 500 ladies in the audience responded with loud applause to all our dances, and afterward we heard "the highlight of my day" and "best entertainment we had this afternoon."

Better than their fashion show? Yay!

At each performance we were met by at least one obstacle, but thanks to Jean and Bernie's pep talks backstage, we rose to the occasion. Sometimes we received unexpected pleasant results.

When the Community Women in Action organization sponsored a benefit performance one afternoon, we expected to see all adult faces in the audience. But at the moment we arrived, we learned that mostly teens were in the auditorium seats.

Oh, dear! Will they make fun of older ladies dancing to music they never heard of? Will they be bored?

Our fears were allayed when they began whistling and cheering from the moment we entered with our kicks and continued throughout the program. We discovered afterward that these youths were members of Job Corps who had come from dysfunctional families and lived on the Tohono Oodham Reservation. During that half-hour with them, they spurred us on to do our ultimate best, and I hope we did the same for them.

One of our instructors taught us a dance we called "Acappella." It took several months to make our taps sound unified since we could not rely on music accompaniment. Jean put on her creative hat and offered this proposal at one of our practices.

"Let's get into University of Arizona's spirit for their upcoming big game. Since we'll soon be performing again for the Shriners, I suggest we wear U.

of A. Victory shirts and do "Acappella."

The evening of the Shriners show, 200 folks in the audience sat quietly and offered polite applause at the end of each dance. However, U. of A. basketball fans went wild when we entered on stage and they saw the lettering on our tee shirts. During "Acappella" we yelled out chants of "Wildcats!" "U. of A.!" "Bear Down!," and a huge roaring "Yes!" at the conclusion. That woke up the audience for the rest of the show.

During that program, several of our dancers who called themselves "The Blues Sisters," made their debut, and they were a hit. Dressed in black suits and white hats, they mimed to the music of "Minnie the Moocher," while inviting the audience to respond by repeating after them.

From then on, they became a staple toward the conclusion of each show, giving the rest of us time to put on our "Stars and Stripes" costumes for the final number.

Several challenges occurred at the Skyline Country Club where we were to perform before the Tucson Arthritis Support League at their spring tea and fashion show. Three times we changed dressing rooms so we could move closer to the stage, no easy feat. Carrying our costumes, shoes and accessories in our arms, we traipsed after Jean who led the way through a kitchen, down a long walkway, through a warehouse-like structure, out onto a windy patio and back inside. We set up in two different places before finally squeezing into a curtained-off dressing area to be shared with the fashion show models.

Gosh, I hope I didn't drop anything along the way.

Once on stage, we posed for Jean to introduce us. Suddenly, I moved my arm and discovered that the sequins on the dancer's sleeve next to me was intertwined with the sequins on my sleeve. We could not separate our arms, figuratively becoming Siamese twins. What to do? Bernie came to the rescue. Sitting back of us with her sound equipment, she jumped up and managed to separate our sleeves by breaking a connecting thread with her teeth, and once divided, we went happily on with the show.

To paraphrase from the song "Life Upon the Wicked Stage," it is not all that we starlets believe it to be, either on or behind the stage. Yes, it is fun to play dress-up in costumes as we did in our youth, to smear our faces with make-up, to master each dance, and to perform a near-flawless performance. Hearing statements such as "Unbelievable!" "You knew your steps," and "Loved your smiles" were also rewarding.

When I danced, at times I felt out of myself, larger and more beautiful. For a few minutes on stage I was heroic and powerful. This awesome sensation was mine for the taking. So I grin and bear the crowded and sometimes wretched dressing rooms and dance upon those wicked stage surfaces. The dancers might moan and groan out of Jean's hearing of course, but when she announces a new booking, we rush to the sign-up book, eager to shine again on that so-called wicked stage.

A week later, we competed against dance schools at the Burger Performing Arts Theater, sponsored by the Spotlight Dance Cup. This time we were on a wonderfully large one with a smooth surface.

After the show, all performers came to the stage and sat on stools to hear the awards. It seemed a long time before we heard the Hot Flashes name.

Oh great! We are receiving first and second prize ribbons for the dances we did, and a certificate for "Best Smile."

But, wait, there was one more. "And the top score goes to -- drum roll please -- the Hot Flashes." Jean proudly stepped up to the emcee to receive a two-foot-tall trophy.

Life upon this not-so-wicked stage treated us well.

Most of our dances took six months to prepare, to master the steps, adjust to the changing of formations, and to finally polish the completed dance before Jean presented it to the public. We never knew how a routine might be accepted, and that was the case with "Heaven Hop." Dressed in nun habits and pulling up our skirts to display red garters might offend devout Catholics.

No need to worry. While performing at the Holy Trinity Monastery, we took a chance on that number. When we reached the point in the dance where we surprised or thought we might have shocked some, the priests and nuns in the audience reacted with peals of laughter. One nun was laughing so hard that tears ran down her cheeks.

A month later, we were on stage at Our Mother of Sorrows Church doing the nun dance for 550 Knights of Columbus who had arrived from all parts of the country for a golf tournament. It was their "Get Acquainted Night", so we let them get acquainted with our notorious dance. Those Catholics roared at "Heaven Hop." That settled all our misgivings. From then on, "Heaven Hop" became a regular on our dancing schedule for all audiences.

After being on our best behavior at the previous two shows, except, of course, when we showed off those red garters, we decided to loosen up and head off to the wild-west. We saddled up our autos and hit the trail to Old Tucson Studios. This western theme park was set up for stagecoach rides, cowboy gun fights, and old-time entertainment.

After an introductory tour of the grounds riding in stagecoaches, we were dropped off at the Grand Palace Hotel and Saloon. The dancers entered through swinging doors to the performing stage where we were scheduled for three shows, the first beginning at 12:30 p.m. and the last at 4:00 p.m.

First, we had to deal with a small stage. We were so crowded that some of the dancers on stage were hidden by the side curtains. The scenic backdrop of mountains and trees, though rather dark, did enhance our colorful costumes.

Our dressing areas backstage were cramped and hot on that May afternoon. I had laid out my costumes on a table in front of a door. To avoid being hit by someone suddenly opening the door, I had to jump back and forth while in the process of pulling on a costume or slipping into a shoe.

Because all four groups had mastered a wide variety of dances, Jean was able to schedule a different set of numbers for each of the three performances. Between shows we rested and recuperated for an hour backstage.

"Okay, ladies, are you ready?"

Jean always referred to us as 'ladies' or 'women.' When anyone, including our own dancers, addressed us as 'girls', she sternly corrected them right then.

I agree with her. People mean well. Perhaps they want to make us feel we're young little girls again playing dress up, putting on makeup and showing off our tap dancing skills.

"Entertainers One, you're on!" We dashed out the back door, tiptoed over large gravel under hot sun, then, through another door. From that direction, stage right, we entered to begin our dance.

We played to a full house at the first two shows, but the crowd dwindled at the third and final one. We were exhausted and famished when the three shows were over. We had eaten only a few grapes since breakfast. However, besides Old Tucson Studios paying the studio $500 for a day's entertainment, we each were rewarded with free meal tickets for a barbecued dinner at their chuck wagon on the premises.

We were truly on our high horses riding home. But little did we know that we were about to rise to even greater heights just three months later.

CHAPTER ELEVEN
A COMMERCIAL VIDEO PRODUCTION

"Dancing is communication, so speak clearly and beautifully."

August 12, 1997 - the day our dance studio transformed into a television studio.

This came about not only because of Jean's vision, but because she also had a backbone that gave strength to her wishbone.

"Hey, Bernie, I have an idea. What do you think might happen if I called our Health Partners insurance and asked them if they would be interested in using our Hot Flashes in a commercial?"

"Go ahead and try it Jean. I think our dancers would be ideal to promote their health insurance."

So Jean made the call. Health Partners was not only interested, they followed through and made Jean's idea a reality the day they brought a dozen workers and scores of equipment into our On Broadway studio. They drove vans, trucks and a catering vehicle into our back alley by 6:30 a.m. In that alley, which we only used to dump garbage into cans, they set up tables laden with fresh fruits and sweet rolls for the crew. Plates of goodies were carried up the back stairs for the dancers.

Two makeup ladies set to work on us immediately and touched us up during the day. Cosmetics applied were more subdued than we wore for our performances.

The crew included two directors, a cameraman, a stage designer, photographers, equipment operators and the two makeup artists. One man was charged with the single responsibility to turn off the air coolers and fans during the taping. It warmed up mighty fast on that hot August day. Equipment was lifted by a cherry picker and then transferred into our studio. The cherry picker remained on the flat roof of our building to deflect the sun's rays. They came prepared.

At 8:30 a.m. they began filming our "Acappella" dance. Twelve dancers dressed in black dance shorts, hot pink blouses, black heels and black hats performed the complete dance several times. Then they took several shots of specific parts, especially of the ending, focusing on our legs and feet.

Oh my goodness, I'm tired of all this repetition. When those fans are off, it is so hot. I must not be distracted by the crew's activities. I can't help watching that hefty-sized man pushing the camera back and forth on a riding dolly. Amazing what they will go through to make a commercial.

Green and maroon curtains provided our background during the taping. Costumes draped over chairs, tap shoes propped up, hats set around, a trophy and a photo displayed, all arranged behind us to show off our dance studio.

We dancers held up quite well during those hours of taping, even Eileen, who had fainted in the coffee room prior to starting. Later much time was spent rearranging the backdrop for the individual interviews of dancers who were members of Health Partners. These conversations between an insurance representative and a dancer were inserted throughout the commercial. At one of the interviews, dressed in practice clothes, we moved to music in the background, removing our shoes so as not to make a sound.

They broke for lunch, and we headed down to the alley where we were treated to a complete gourmet meal from appetizers to dessert and all the drinks we wanted. In fact, they later carried up an ice chest full of sodas for us. We were treated like Hollywood stars. One dancer needed a toothbrush and one of the crew went out and bought her one.

The crew departed about four o'clock, but not before they cleaned up everything including the bathrooms. That one day they spent ten thousand dollars plus giving each of us fifty dollars. More money would be spent on turning those tapes into a finished product, a 30-second video. I was so impressed how they conducted their jobs, how efficient they were and how well they cooperated as a team.

When the film was completed at their video productions studio, we were each given a copy. For one year that video was shown around the clock on various channels throughout the state of Arizona.

A month later, Health Partners requested that we attend a photo session at the Tim Fuller Studio in downtown Tucson. Entering an old building that looked as though it had been standing there since Tucson began, we climbed the steps to the second floor. The studio was as plain as Lance-Fairchild's upscale photo studio in town was fancy. All we could see was a bunch of photo equipment spread around in a well-worn large room. Tim Fuller, a middle-aged man, dressed as casually as he might be in his own home. I looked down to see if he had slippers on. He welcomed and directed us to a small storage area where we could slip into our "Acappella" costumes.

The same two makeup artists who had been there for the filming of the commercial at our studio were there to pretty us up. Refreshments of donuts, muffins and juice provided energy to take us through the long and stressful morning ahead.

These Health partners think of everything.

Tim Fuller was as humorous as he was skillful. He arranged us in various positions, all the while acting complimentary and tactful. "Anyone willing to get up and down on their knees?" Tim asked.

Helen, Joanie and I volunteered. That is how we managed to be in the front row of the photograph that was chosen. Dozens of shots were taken of us in different positions in rapid order. One, two, three, snap. One, two, three, snap. Three hours later the photo session was over. I now understand what models go through. Not the easy plush life of posing for a minute and then they collect their pay.

Later when we saw our picture on a flyer advertising Health Partners for Seniors, we knew the insurance company had selected the right photographer. The colorful flyers appeared in Sunday newspapers for a year and black and white circulars were inserted in daily publications.

Paperwork? What's that?

— Jean Johnson, The Hot Flashes
senior dance group

HealthPartners for Seniors
A Medicare + Choice Plan from HealthPartners Health Plans

Figure 17 Flyer for HealthPartners Health Plans

With the exciting experience of the commercial and the photo session behind us, it was time to return to what the Hot Flashes did best, tap dancing and performing for others. First on the agenda, the Home Show which always drew a big crowd. Just before we were scheduled to go on, two men on stage were showing live desert critters. As they came off, while we were waiting in the wings, they gave us a close view of their rattlesnakes and Gila monster. If we already had stage jitters that just made us shake a little more.

All seats were filled for our show and the folks who hired us wanted us back for the next two days. We could not accept the third day because we were due to perform at the Botanical Gardens for the La Fiesta de los Chiles.

We should have remained at the Home Show.

Here's what happened. Arriving at noon, we crowded into one small dressing room. Just as we had all our outfits set out and dressed in our first costume, Jean announced, "We are moving to the outdoor main stage."

So we gathered our belongings and paraded through the grounds in our costumes only to learn that the raised wooden stage was terribly dilapidated with pieces of wood sticking out between floor boards. If we didn't gouge our feet on the stage, then the stage itself might have collapsed under our weight. Also, there was no place to change costumes. Back we traipsed through all the people who were milling around in the gardens. We were hauling suitcases, stools and costumes, looking like a long lost caravan.

Back in that original cramped dressing room, we laid out our costumes and prepared to dance on smooth stepping stones in a small space in one of their buildings. Since there were no seats, we played to a standing room only crowd. Some folks gazed at us through the windows. They moved along with our music and gave us a standing ovation. What else could they do? Besides, a good song and dance makes the listener dance also. It was the longest applause we had ever received.

On certain occasions Jean had good reasons to be upset with us. Frequently some of the eager Hot Flashes arrived two hours before the scheduled performance. They used the time to bustle around checking out the stage and dressing room. Later, as some of us trickled in, we were greeted with, "Wait till you see the stage. We'll never fit on it. And there is only one tiny dressing room. We talked to the person in charge and told her that we cannot dance under those conditions." Then Jean and Bernie arrived, furious that these dancers had taken it upon themselves to complain to the person who hired us.

"There is only one director", Jean admonished them, "and that is me. Only Bernie and I will discuss any stage or dressing room problems with the lady here. Your only responsibilities are to arrive one hour ahead of a performance, arrange your costumes and dance. But you are not, damn it, to complain to anybody about the conditions. That is my job. We don't need more than one director and I am it," she emphasized by jabbing her chest.

Somehow Jean, with Bernie's assistance, always solved the problems, whether it meant removing a few dancers in certain numbers on a crowded stage or helping us find a place to dress when dressing rooms were crowded. Everyone involved did whatever it took to provide the best show.

January 1998 began with a second sea voyage when the Hot Flashes entered the All-America Cruise Competition again. This time we were gone for one week, visiting several Mexican ports.

The worst part of this trip was to dance while the ship was moving. Two years before, the competition was held while the ship was in the Ensenada port. It is bad enough to walk and keep one's balance while the ship is rocking and rolling. But try tap dancing in a competition when you are striving for a gold medal.

Oh me! I'm losing my balance just standing in line ready to go on.

As it turned out, no one fell on that moving stage and all of our Hot Flash groups together won five gold and five silver medals.

One day during the cruise, we had just returned to the ship from a Matzatlan tour at 4:30 p.m. only to learn that the Hot Flashes should sign up by 5:00 p.m. to be one of the eight acts to participate in that night's talent show in the Atlantis Lounge. We met the deadline, and we were first to perform with our "Happy Feet" number.

I don't think we will win. By the time they get to act number eight, they will have forgotten about us.

I was so wrong. Perhaps the loud and boisterous applause determined first prize for us. We were presented with three bottles of champagne and a small gold trophy of the ship.

Back in Tucson from that competition cruise, we resumed our local performances. A month later we played for 300 Holiday Ramblers at the Pima County Fairgrounds. Stepping through mud puddles from the recent rains, we entered a huge building where we danced on a raised but rough and bumpy stage.

Oh, it's so-o-o cold in here.

Several mishaps occurred during the show. My wedding ring flew off to the back of the stage during our "Thoroughly Modern Millie" dance, but I retrieved it as we went off. Judy dropped her tambourine while doing "Patricia", but recovered it during the dance when we moved into our clump. Lois fell on her knee as she was running down the steps of the stage. As always, Lois kept going, dancing with a very sore knee. Nothing stopped her. We were told that if we stumbled to make it appear part of the dance.

The very responsive audience overlooked any flaws in our presentation and gave us a standing ovation. It might have been cold when we began, but we certainly warmed up that audience. One lady told Jean she saw us at Palm Springs. She was referring to the annual Palm Springs Follies put on by retired professionals. Jean did not tell her differently. Let her think we were those accomplished ladies.

It was time again for the annual St. Patrick's Day parade. The Hot Flashes participated as usual. For a change, it was cool, cloudy and windy, so I did not have to worry about my eyelashes falling off from sweat dribbling down my face.

We were positioned between two fire trucks during the parade. The one in back honked periodically startling us out of our skins. It drowned out our music too. Still it was fun and we won third prize out of ninety entries. That is not bad.

Figure 18 The Hot Flashes in the St. Patrick's Day Parade

In the days following the parade, the Hot Flashes continued to be in great demand, partially due to the commercial we had made. The following are highlights and fiascos from some of our performances.

At the Villa Capri Mobile home Park, we tried out our rousing new entrance as we strutted in to the music of "That's Entertainment." The crowd received us with a large applause, so that opening replaced "New York, New York" from then on. During our final dance, one of the dancers came out with a yellow tag stuck to her band hat as she danced to "Stars and Stripes." Later back stage she poked fun of herself. "I was just trying to be Minnie Pearl."

The Shriners invited us back for a third year in a row. Our show began with a shaky start. As we strutted through the audience to "That's Entertainment", the sound system sputtered and failed. Jean, reaching the stage, grabbed the microphone, but it too had died. She shouted to the packed crowd our usual introduction.

I wonder if those people at the back can hear anything she is saying. If they only catch the words "Hot Flashes" they may think she is talking about women's menopause problems.

Once the sound system was up and running we showed them what Hot Flashes really meant; women of a certain age, team tapping with vigor. During "Patricia", Lois caught her tambourine on Carolyn's skirt, and my tambourine stuck to my skirt too.

Golly, I can't get this thing loose. Oh, finally! Hope I didn't tear my skirt.

A man in the front row had a coughing choking fit which was disturbing and alarming for us. But the lady next to him gave him a cough drop to quiet him down. Near the close of the show, we frantically ran all over back stage searching for the flag for "Stars and Stripes". Someone finally spotted it leaning against the wall in a small adjoining room. The flag was brought on just in time.

A few months earlier we had introduced a new lively dance to "Sing, Sing, Sing." The swaying fringes on our costumes enhanced that dance as we quickly changed formations. At one place in the dance we tapped into a clump performing intertwining complicated moves. This usually brought on applause from the audience. However, at the Old Pueblo Mustang Club that maneuver in the middle of the routine not only brought a lengthy applause, but the spectators jumped to their feet. One man yelled, "Bravo" and others called out "You're fabulous!"

Figure 19 Dancing to "Sing, Sing, Sing"

Before the same audience, Jean made an embarrassing or possibly an intended gaffe. To fill in the time while we were changing, she related a tale about the Hot Flashes while on a recent Mexican cruise. She told about a woman who came up to her and asked if we were an advertisement for condoms. At that the audience roared even though it did not make sense. "Oh, I meant to say menopause", Jean added. Too late, the damage was done.

They loved it, but it probably would not have gone over at St. David's monastery.

An extremely difficult challenge occurred at the University of Arizona for the Staff Advisory Council. We performed in a lecture hall similar to an amphitheater with rows of tiered seats. Dancing on the stage was like dancing on a ledge. The front edge was a sheer drop off at least six feet down. Scary! To add to the problem the stage was only eight feet deep and the highly polished tiles were terribly slippery. Luckily no one fell off the front, but Maggie in the back row slipped and broke her hand, which sadly took her out of dancing for a while. We did enjoy a rousing crowd, especially during "Acappella" when we wore our University of Arizona basketball shirts as we had done for the Shriners.

On a very sad note, Gloria Lee, the dancer Jean had met in a tap class for youths seven years before and was the first to join Jean in what would become the Hot Flashes, passed away from a severe illness on March 11, 1998.

To honor her on the day of her funeral, we dancers gathered in the parking lot dressed in our Hot Flashes tee shirts, black trousers and tap shoes. Then we filed in two-by-two, doing the military times step. Each of us carried a long stemmed rose to place in front of photographs and memorabilia on display. We sat in the second row reserved for us. During the service Jean gave a beautifully moving speech, recalling Hot Flash experiences with Gloria. At the conclusion of the service, we dance-stepped in formation out to the parking lot.

It was a privilege to honor Gloria in that way. When she had become too ill to continue dancing with us, she came into the studio for the last time, deposited all her costumes and departed quickly, so broken hearted was she.

It is too bad she couldn't have continued with us to experience the exciting years ahead. Jean's big dream for the Hot Flashes was about to come true.

Leona Claire Fuller

CHAPTER TWELVE
THE NEW YORK EXPERIENCE

"The Hot Flashes Take New York"

It's a go! Can't believe it. We're on our way to New York City, all expenses paid by Pharmaton Natural Health Products.

Pharmaton, a Connecticut pharmaceutical company, sent letters to women's dance groups around the nation asking if they were interested in performing in New York, all expenses paid. If so, they requested the group to mail in an audition tape.

Jean did not waste a minute submitting a video of one of the Hot Flashes' shows. "Favorite Son" was on the tape, the dance with us sitting on stools during part of the number, crossing and uncrossing our legs. Pharmaton was planning to promote leg health week for their product Venastat. Their slogan was "The Great American Crossout" meaning crossing your legs was bad for circulation. Our dance routine fit their slogan perfectly, so we were chosen to go to the Big Apple.

The morning of departure found the Hot Flashes at the Tucson airport dressed in hot pink Hot Flashes tee shirts. We lined up side-by-side, kicking to the music of "New York, New York" as a cameraman from Channel 4 took pictures of us. Passengers in the airport applauded.

What a sendoff!

We boarded the plane with carry-ons in one hand and stools in the other. No sooner were we settled in our seats, the attendants informed us there was a mechanical problem. Off the plane we went, hauling all our belongings. This inconvenience was minor compared to the rest of our journey that day.

An hour and a half delay at Tucson airport caused us to miss our connecting flight at the Dallas-Fort Worth airport. The airline personnel struggled to work us onto another flight, causing us to change lines four times before they found enough seats for all of us.

In 1998, food was furnished on all domestic flights. The lunch served onboard that day was hot chicken sandwiches. Those of us seated at the back waited patiently, ravenously hungry and smelling all those pleasant cooking aromas. By the time the flight attendants reached us they had run out of sandwiches, so a bag of chips and a cookie had to suffice.

Preparing to descend into New York City, the captain announced that thunderstorms around La Guardia airport prevented a landing. After circling for about an hour, the plane headed to Philadelphia to refuel. Even there, we flew above the airport for a while before receiving clearance to land.

We stayed on the plane while they refueled, about half an hour. Surprise! Sack lunches were brought aboard for those who did not receive food earlier. The flight then returned and landed at New York's La Guardia airport at 8:30 p.m. instead of the previously designated 4:00 p.m. arrival time.

Mark, the Brooklyn Bus Company driver, was there to meet and drive us to the Roosevelt Hotel where we unloaded our bags. No sooner had we remove them than we were told to reload the bags and go to the Hudson Street Restaurant. Our driver got lost in the dark. He made so many turns that if there had been another, we might have landed in the Hudson River.

When we finally found the long sought after restaurant, a woman rushed out to inform us, "A mistake has been made. You are not supposed to eat here. You have to return to the Roosevelt Hotel." So back we drove, unloaded bags and enjoyed a full course dinner at eleven o'clock at night. After dinner, Sandra and Bryan, the public relations representatives from Pharmaton, briefed us on how to conduct an interview and answer questions about Venastat and the Great American Crossout.

I am so tired I can hardly concentrate on what they are saying.

I came back to life when we each were given four hundred dollars for food expenses while in New York City.

Everyone dropped into bed after 1:00 a.m., but not for long. A wake-up call at 4:00 a.m. was the signal to arise, quickly apply our make-up and dress in long-sleeved white and purple pullover shirts furnished by Pharmaton with the Venastat insignia on the front. It showed legs crossed with a dark line drawn through them. We had brought purple shorts and matching hat to go with the shirt, which we were expected to wear every day to advertise leg health week and their product Venastat.

Forty-five minutes after the early wake-up call, we gathered in the lobby waiting for taxis to drive us to the NBC studio. We were scheduled to dance on the local New York Today Show. A taxi strike hit the city that very day. Somehow enough taxis were rounded up to take all sixteen of us to the building that housed the NBC studio. We marched upstairs to the studio, guided by our Pharmaton representatives, only to learn our dance performance had been bumped by the taxi strike problems, that controversy taking priority over our presentation.

So the Hot Flashes troupe trudged across the street where crews were setting up for the national Today Show. Three long hours we stood as a group behind a railing without food or drink, hoping to be on this well-known show. Gradually other tourists gathered behind the fence with their hometown signs and messages angling to be seen. Periodically the hosts of the Today Show, Matt Lauer, Anne Curry and Sarah James, substituting for Katie Couric, walked out of the NBC building and circled around near the crowds with cameras following. They seemed to ignore us until during their final round, our purple outfits caught their attention. Jean was interviewed and she did so well it brought cheers, tears and thrills, not only to her dancers but to the Venastat representatives.

Sarah James called us the "Great American Hot Flashes." Matt Lauer cracked, "You're the Rockettes in prison" referring to our legs poking through the bars of the fence. At last we had been noticed. After the show we did a triple times step for Ann Curry as she watched from inside the fence with a wide smile. She then leaned across to have her photograph taken with us. Finally, the Hot Flashes had a chance to dance, albeit for an audience of one after the Today Show.

Now the ladies were ready to return to the hotel for some nourishment and a well-earned rest. We walked across the street to the park area of the Rockefeller Center to await a van from the hotel. Never letting a minute go to waste, we dancers practiced our "Acappella" number on the walkway, which drew a crowd. Showing off our stuff was great fun until stopped by the police. "Sorry ladies, no dancing in the park unless you have a permit. You will have to move on."

Figure 20 The Hot Flashes posing at Rockefeller Center

Oh well, we almost made it through that dance.

In the years to follow, Jean liked to tell our audiences how we danced at Rockefeller Center, but the police ran us out of there.

The next day was one of the greatest days of my life. The Hot Flashes performed in New York City. I still have trouble believing it. On this beautiful sunny day, the group was transported by van to Columbus Circle. A large 16 by 24-foot raised stage was set outdoors. Pharmaton sent out technicians to film a Venastat commercial of us. For one hour we sat on stools for a taping session, crossing and uncrossing our legs, putting our legs up on the backs of chairs, jumping up to do the times step, sitting back down and twirling ankles and tapping toes.

I am so hot sitting all this time in the sun in this long-sleeved warm shirt. I'm frustrated trying to get my leg up on that chair.

Passersby stopped to watch us and even applauded when the director indicated that we got it right for the cameras. Once the taping was finally over, I sat quietly on my stool, looking around in amazement at all the tall buildings, the buses and cars rushing by with people peering through their windows at us.

Are the Hot Flashes really in New York City and receiving all this attention?

Then I looked down and noticed Hilda found an empty grocery cart and placed our handbags inside and was pushing it around the stage area. Literally the perfect bag lady! Some man came up to her later and warned her that she might have taken some homeless person's cart.

At 12:30 p.m. the show began to the tune of ambulance sirens screeching through the streets. The Hot Flashes ran through six dances, beginning with the domino effect of uncrossing our legs, then straight into "Favorite Son." More crowds were forming. Buses and cars slowed down as passengers turned their heads to watch us. I like to think the performance actually stopped traffic. Even though we were mature women, we often received this kind of attention and compliments on how great our legs looked. Thank goodness for those shimmery light toast tights.

The big bosses from Pharmaton praised us highly and told us that they had no idea we could draw such a crowd. "We'd like to see you do "Favorite Son" one more time", which we did. Then the ambulance sirens sounded again. Perfect timing.

Channel 7 of ABC televised our show and interviewed Jean and Judy, one of the dancers who was a native New Yorker. Both did superb jobs answering the questions while the Hot Flashes posed behind them.

After many photo taking sessions, some by newspapers, we sat on our stools and devoured sack lunches. It tasted so good after a hard day's work of dancing, crossing and uncrossing legs.

Jean introduced our dance team to a Rockette who was passing by, a lovely tall dark-haired woman who had seen part of our show. She appeared impressed and encouraged us to keep dancing. After all, the Rockettes were our idols. We even borrowed some of their dance steps in striving to be like them, at a slower pace of course.

Back at the hotel we gathered in the lounge to see ourselves on television. There the Hot Flashes were on ABC's Channel 7 during the 7:00 p.m. newscast. We let out a shout when we viewed parts of our performance. "Hey, look at all those legs. We look great."

So exciting! Imagine, I'm on TV in New York City.

The next morning one of our dancers came running into my room waving a copy of the *New York Times*. "Our photo is in this paper." We tore downstairs and bought out the papers from the gift shop and from several newsstands in the vicinity. Page two in the Metro section featured a large black and white photograph at the top of the page showing us kicking our legs during one of the dances. It was a great advertisement for the Venastat folks, but it also brought the Hot Flashes into the national spotlight.

The New York Times

Copyright © 1998 The New York Times   *NEW YORK, SATURDAY, MAY 23, 1998* $1 beyond the greater New York metrop

Nancy Siesel/The New York Times

Flashing a Lot of Legs

Members of the Hot Flashes Dance Troupe from Tucson, Ariz., performed yesterday at Columbus Circle in Manhattan. The tap dancers, who range in age from 56 to 74, performed as part of a campaign encouraging women to stop crossing their legs, a practice doctors say contributes to varicose veins.

Figure 21 The Hot Flashes performing at Columbus Circle, New York City

The second stirring event of the day was a trip to Ford Center for Performing Arts to see "Ragtime", the musical. Tickets were provided by our sponsors at a total cost of $1,034. Seats were reserved for us in the first two rows of the balcony. It was a stunning production with an abundance of ragtime melodies depicting conflicts during the early 1900s between blacks and whites, industrialists and union leaders. The show featured historical figures such as Henry Ford, Booker T. Washington, J. Pierpont Morgan and Admiral Robert Peary.

The fourth day, May 24, our romantic dream world trip came to an end. We expected to be staying longer because our sponsors were attempting to line up appearances on the Rosie O'Donnell and the New York Today Show.

But, we did not hear from them, Jean was not feeling well and some of the dancers were tired and ready to return home.

The Hot Flash members would not say goodbye to New York City without taking beautiful memories home of the excellent hotel accommodations, transportation, gourmet meals, television appearances and attending a Broadway musical. Above all, we treasured the public and professional recognition of our dancing abilities.

Departing for the airport, Bernie captured the twin towers of the World Trade Center on film from the moving bus as it crossed the bridge. Just three years later, those city landmarks would be destroyed by terrorist acts.

The trip to Tucson was smooth and uneventful compared to the chaotic trip to New York. We arrived ahead of schedule at 9:00 p.m. Beaming husbands and children were there to greet us. Some of the Hot Flashes from Entertainers Two were displaying large signs made by Carolyn's husband Charlie, which read "Welcome Back from New York" and "You Made It to the Top."

Such a wonderful welcome. I only wish we could have taken all the Hot Flashes performing groups.

Later we learned that entire trip cost the Pharmaton Company $100,000. We were worth it to them in publicity. Years later when the Hot Flashes dance troupe was no more, that company called again wanting us back. Truly a great compliment.

CHAPTER THIRTEEN
FIESTA BOWL PARADE

"We cannot stay long on the mountaintop, then we must come down and deal with the needs of the valley." Evelyn Underhill

How do you come down from the top of the mountain after you have high-kicked across the stage at Columbus Circle in New York City, appeared on the Today Show and made the *New York Times*?

"Here's my answer to that", Jean declared, "We'll bring Broadway to Tucson". And indeed we did. At one of the Hot Flashes' next shows one spectator remarked, "I've seen Broadway shows and you are a match for them."

There was no time to rest on our laurels as the dancers all returned to lessons and practice. The choreographer dictated the steps and the tap dancers worked on them over and over until they perfected those steps. The instructor called out, "One more time", which translated into ten more times. No one complained. After all, great dancing comes from the love and passion for dance, as well as technique. Tucson audiences were waiting for quality performances, and just twelve days later we were back on stage to deliver.

Jean wanted to add more variety to our shows. She previously included the "Blues Sisters" in the lineups. Now she added Group Two's tambourine routine. Sitting on stools, beating tambourines, they swung the instruments in circles, threw them in the air and caught them, all to the tempo of

"Music, Music, Music." It took days of practice and battered arms to achieve those tricky movements.

Figure 22 Group 2 posed to begin their tambourine routine

It is encouraging for a performer to have a lively audience, but sometimes it can go too far. One stifling hot July afternoon, while entertaining the Job Corps, in a non-air conditioned building, some teens screamed so loudly throughout the show we could not hear the music. Not good for tip-tap-toe tapping dancers. That's a mouthful.

Backstage more serious problems occurred. With not even a fan, excessive perspiration made it a struggle to wiggle into costumes or pull long-sleeved gloves over sweaty arms. But worse, one dancer became overheated and passed out, slumping to the floor just before the last number. We cooled her with dampened paper towels till the paramedics arrived and revived her. The rest of us still shaking from that incident, rushed out belatedly for "Stars and Stripes".

Hot Flashes bookings often came in groups because Jean rarely turned down a request. One three day weekend, we hot-footed it through five shows. We performed three times for the Oktoberfest, and one each for a Naval Reunion and the 487th Bomb Group.

A favorite show of mine was for the Elderhostel folks who attended from around the country. All we could see were smiling faces in the audience. I noticed one woman, her cupped hand under her chin shaking her head in awe as she intensely gazed at us. When the dancers began "Sing, Sing, Sing", facing to the back and swinging our hips, one man called out, "I don't know if my pacemaker can take it." That drew much laughter from the audience and controlled snickers from the performers on stage.

At the close of each year Jean reserved a hotel banquet room for a Hot Flashes' Christmas luncheon. It gave dancers a chance to chat, to exchange gifts and to see each other in dressy street clothes instead of tee shirts, leotards and dance tights. Not much time for any of that socializing during dance classes. Jean, standing at the podium, addressed the group first by reviewing highlights of the past year. Then she rallied us with a pep talk for the coming year.

"We've got something big coming up. Instead of starting 1999 with a cruise or the state Senior Olympics, we will be providing entertainment during half-time for the University of Arizona Women's Basketball game."

Sure enough, the 4th of January found the troupe at McKale Center presenting a new version of "St. Louis Blues March." We changed into our "Stars and Stripes" costumes in the men's locker room under the watch of past champions' pictures posted on the "Wildcat Wall of Fame."

The crowds in the bleachers cheered us on as we marched across the floor. The music began, the dancers moved perfectly through the ever changing formations till we entered the circle.

Oh dear, the person ahead of me slipped into a different spot. What shall I do? Now I am behind the wrong person, on the wrong foot and I've lost the timing. Quick, move into the final lineup. Oh gee, I'm kicking with the wrong leg. All those hours of practice, and I am blowing it.

Comments afterward to the Hot Flashes included, "You made a great impression," "Best entertainment they've ever had," and "We want you back." They must not have seen my mistakes. Unless they were focused on only one dancer like me out of twenty-four. As Jean instructed, "Just keep moving and smiling." It really worked.

Challenges kept coming for the Hot Flashes. There was always another first time for everything. Electricity was the culprit at the Rincon Country West R.V. Park. As we were happily dancing to the music of "Happy Feet," the lights went out, along with the music. Folks in charge lit flashlights and candles as we stayed in our positions. Jean announced, "If the lights aren't on in twenty minutes, we'll give you a rain check, or rather a power check." Ten minutes later the lights were on for the rest of the show.

Electricity problems followed us to the very next performance. At the Home Show the lights stayed on, but the sound system failed while Group Two was in the middle of their "Cerveza" dance. They continued, "Acappella"-like and never missed a beat. Another group followed with

"Sing, Sing, Sing", completing the entire dance without music, our taps in harmony. That requires listening carefully to each other's taps, sending sound messages with their feet.

The sound system was restored for the remainder of the show. "I am so impressed that you dancers handled that power failure so well," Jean told us after the show. "The Hot Flashes can handle any situation."

Sometimes when one climbs to the top, as our troupe did in New York, we can look around and see there are still other peaks waiting for us beyond. One day that opportunity arrived in the mail.

"Bernie come in here!" Jean yelled from her office at the studio. "Wait till you read this. It's from the Fiesta Bowl parade committee in Phoenix. They want us to audition for their December parade. How many years have we applied to be in that parade?"

"At least three or four," Bernie responded, "and they've always sent back a letter saying, Sorry, we can't use you this time. Try again next year."

"I can't wait to tell the women when they arrive at the studio this morning," Jean said, still shaking her head in disbelief.

As soon as the dancers filed in and put on their tap shoes to prepare for the lesson, Jean made her big announcement. "It looks as though we will be in the Fiesta Bowl parade."

I am in awe. Wait, what is she saying?

"Before we are accepted, we have to audition. Can't just send in a video. So that means we have to create a special routine and hit that street again to drill. That includes all four groups and many practices."

Fortunately The Hot Flashes only had one booking that month, which gave us time to focus on the parade instead of performances. After every class, when we were already tired, we spent another hour marching and dancing around a couple of streets and using tambourines as part of the routine.

Four weeks before the parade we were on our way by chartered bus to Phoenix, one hundred twenty miles north, for the audition. The parade chairman and two others greeted us at the Northern Baptist Church's huge parking lot. Dressed in parade costumes of fringe covered pink leotards, we marched and danced around the parking lot to music.

After only five minutes, the parade committee stopped us. The chairman announced, "I am pleased, you passed the audition and we'll see you on parade day. One suggestion, you might want to eliminate the shuffles since it could slow you down."

We boarded the bus, changed back into street clothes and stopped for lunch to celebrate on the way home. A great day for the Hot Flashes. A long drive for a five minute audition, but it was worth it. Jean Johnson sent out a news release to the *Arizona Daily Star* with the headline, Tucson Hot Flashes to March in the Fiesta Bowl Parade December 31, 1999.

The Hot Flashes rode to Phoenix in a chartered bus a day before the parade and spent the night at the Hyatt Regency Hotel. That would give us a fresh and rested start the next morning for the 11 o'clock parade. We wanted to be our best for the Fiesta Bowl parade, because it was Arizona's largest spectator event.

On the appointed parade day, the bus dropped us off at the same church parking lot where we had auditioned. The costumed dancers lined up in the street by the parking lot and waited two hours in the cold, shivering at times, before moving into the parade line on Central Avenue. Our place was third from the end, with a horse group in front of us. *We better watch where we step.* There were women motorcyclists behind us called the "Hardly Angels."

One last minute instruction from Jean as she called out, "Watch your lines and keep moving. Stay with the group ahead. They don't want us holding up the parade."

Thousands of spectators lined the streets for the three mile route, cheering and applauding the entire way. I heard that the organizers were expecting 400,000 people to attend. The audience especially liked when we paused to hit our hips with the tambourines, the other arm extended above our heads in a sexy move, shouting out, "Woo!" A voice from the crowd shouted out, "You look better than the high-schoolers."

Figure 23 The Hot Flashes dancing in the Fiesta Bowl parade

Three ladies carried the "Hot Flashes" banner. Jean walked behind them and stayed in the parade until our group passed the television cameras. Her stamina was remarkable considering she was in the hospital just two weeks previously for breathing problems. Jean handed the baton to Joyce, one of our competent dancers, and boarded the golf cart that followed behind us, carrying Bernie and Charlie, Carolyn's husband, with the music equipment.

Charlie made a large sign decorated in pink and black theme colors with a picture of a silver dance shoe and our Hot Flashes name above it. Riding atop the golf cart, that sign made a big impression. At least, the crowds and judges knew who the Hot Flashes were.

Figure 24 Charlie in the Fiesta Bowl parade with his Hot Flashes sign

At the end of the parade, when it suddenly came to a halt, my body continued the momentum for a while, even though I was standing still. A strange sensation.

Our longest parade. Three miles. And we made it! Another achievement for the Hot Flashes, dancing through the entire parade route, heads held high and smiles to light up the world.

The energy and beat continued in Tucson for the next two nights, January 1st and 2nd, 2000, as the Hot Flashes performed at the Millennium Extravaganza. The dancers were genuine troupers, tap dancing with blisters, sore feet and tired legs. Excellence was our standard and pushing our bodies to the physical extremes became a daily norm.

January 4th found us at Tucson's City Hall for the sealing of the Millennium Time Capsule. We were attending this special occasion because the Hot Flashes were contributing a pair of gold tap shoes, a Hot Flash tee shirt, a Hot Flashes photograph calendar for the year 2000, and a copy of *Dance Teacher Now* magazine featuring a five-page article about the Hot Flashes to the contents of the capsule.

By this time the Hot Flashes had built up a large repertoire of dances. Through the years some had been retired, a few had been altered and others played to new songs, using the same costumes. For example, the nun sisters, now danced in an energetic gospel number called "Operator."

Although it took about six months to perfect a dance before taking it out, occasionally the dancers struggled with a routine longer, trying to get it right, only to have Jean throw it out. If it did not match her standards of excellence, it was goodbye and good riddance, but always a disappointment to me after all the work we put into it.

The Hot Flashes, by its ninth year, had performed for more than five hundred civic organizations and conventions, and that was not counting manufactured home communities, retirement centers, church groups, private clubs and home shows. The demand for performances continued with the Hot Flashes entertaining at seven different venues since the Fiesta Bowl parade, and it was only six weeks into the New Year.

Then an unusual call came. Jean answered the phone. "You're who? Montage by Marilyn? Yes, yes, I've heard of Oscar Mayer." The voice on the other end was telling Jean that Marilyn had been hired to set up an 80th birthday party for the wife of Oscar Mayer at the Phoenician Hotel in Scottsdale, Arizona. Asking if the Hot Flashes could perform with all expenses paid, including transportation, plus a large compensation for the entertainment.

"Send us details and I'll take it up with our dancers. Then I'll let you know", Jean responded in a business-like tone, covering up the excitement she was feeling. "Bernie, wait till you hear this!"

CHAPTER FOURTEEN
ALASKA CRUISE SHOW

"Success is not final, failure is not fatal; it is the courage to continue that counts." Winston Churchill

The next morning Jean came into the studio humming the Oscar Mayer jingle. "Oh, Bernie, I can't get that tune out of my head."

The women were already in the studio waiting to hear more about Selma's birthday party and full of questions. "When are we going? How are we getting there? What dances will we do?"

"I'll tell you what we are not going to do," Jean answered, "we are not going to sing 'I wish I were an Oscar Mayer wiener.'" We laughed and rolled our eyes to that statement. "The only singing we'll do is the birthday song for Selma. Each group will do one dance, except for "Stars and Stripes", which involves Groups One and Two. I'll answer your other questions later. Now get to work and polish your dances."

Our days were spent preparing for the stage. The dancers had to retain vast amounts of information with music as our only map. Dance is joy and music made visible.

On a Saturday afternoon in February an excited troupe of Hot Flashes departed by bus for Scottsdale, Arizona arriving at the Phoenician Hotel at 5:00 p.m.

I am in awe at the sight of this beautiful hotel surrounded by immaculate grounds and a golf course.

Inside the hotel, we entered the Estrella Theater where workers were bustling around preparing for Selma's 80th birthday party. Large bouquets of red roses decorated the tables and enlarged photographs of Selma and her husband covered the walls.

In contrast to the elaborate banquet hall, the three dimly-lit dressing rooms upstairs behind the stage were barren, except for one table and a few chairs in each room. We set out our costumes, expecting to be performing within the hour. Little did we know that we had a long evening of waiting ahead of us.

We did not go hungry. Sandwiches, cookies and sodas, provided by the hotel staff, filled us up. Dinner for the guests did not begin until 8:00 p.m., at which time they served only the soup. The program was arranged so that each course was served on the half-hour with ballroom dancing, slide shows and entertainment during the intervals.

Back stage, dancers waited in costumes as the clock struck 9:00 p.m., then 10:00 p.m. We were falling asleep, but everyone jumped up when they heard the call, "We are ready for the Hot Flashes."

Out we filed through the tables, doing a parade routine to "When I'm 64." That is only sixteen years from eighty, Selma's age. Close enough. Jean and one of the dancers were selected to carry out a cake in the shape of a hot dog to Selma. That is when our troupe sang "Happy Birthday", but having heard that Selma loved to eat wieners, I would have preferred to sing the Oscar Mayer jingle.

Up on the stage, we performed four dances with the fifth dance down in the center of the banquet room floor. The cheering audience, applauding our every move and yelling "Bravo", now had us fully awake.

Wow! What an audience. Wish we could take them with us.

At the beginning of the show, Bernie was stationed in the sound control booth so she could direct the technicians when to start the music. But she did not like their rude attitude toward her. "Don't you dare touch our equipment. We don't want anything messed up."

Bernie, who probably knew more about sound technology than the two of them together, might have been more understanding if they had been respectful to her. Perhaps they were suspicious of a sixty-five year old woman knowing anything.

After the show the sound technicians changed their tune when they saw the capability of mature women tap dancers. Heard from the control booth, "They're incredible. Are all their dances that fast? The party was dull until they appeared."

Exhausted dancers boarded the bus at midnight, arriving back in Tucson at 3:00 a.m. Pulling my suitcase through the gate of my apartment complex, who did I meet but the newspaper delivery boy making his rounds. He was probably surprised to see me too.

The next afternoon the Hot Flashes performed at the Skyline Country Club in honor of one of our dancer's Golden Anniversary. Exhausted and barely awake, we put on a good show anyway. Then I, and certainly the others, went home and contentedly collapsed into a well-deserved rest.

Two days later we were toe tapping again at a benefit for persons with Alzheimer's and other disabilities. Show performances continued through the months from the St. Patrick's Day Parade to another big production for the Shriners and several reunions and organizations.

Rehearsals at the performance venues were rarely in the group's schedules. We invariably adjusted, adapted, and conquered all conditions, giving the clients and audiences a great show for their money.

No performances were ever the same. We never knew what to expect. In 93 degree heat at the Pima County Fair, we danced in direct sunlight. Hot, sweaty and lightheaded, we dashed back to the dressing room where Ginny, one of our dancers, sprayed us with a cool mist during costume changes. Back out for "Stars and Stripes", when a woman from the audience decided she wanted to get into the act and attempted to dance with us, causing a distraction. It was hard enough to focus on intricate steps in that heat, but at least she was having a good time.

We almost missed the Women in Construction show scheduled at the Sheraton Hotel a year in advance. Bernie took the request and jotted it down in her book, but it was not recorded at the studio.

"Oh my, gosh! Jean, I just looked at our scheduling book. We've got a show to do at 8:00 p.m. tonight.

"What? It's two o'clock now. We better round up as many dancers as we can. Start calling."

On such short notice, the Hot Flashes answered the call. Those women construction workers were a lively bunch, fired up when we appeared on the stage. They loved our performance, but if we had missed that date they might have remembered us as the "Hot Fizzlers."

A more embarrassing episode was the time we showed up for a performance not scheduled. I had taken the call and listed it on our board. But I made the mistake of not checking back with them to verify the date. So, at eight o'clock one morning a large troupe of the dancers arrived at a mobile home park with stage make-up on and costumes in tow only to learn they had not scheduled us. What to do? We returned to our cars and drowned our disappointment at a nearby café.

I feel terrible. This food doesn't help at all. I want to go home and hide.

But I did not stay in hiding for long; not when I heard there was to be another cruise, this time to Alaska for one week. "It is not a competition," Jean reassured us. "Carnival Lines is allowing us to put on our own show. We must still pay our fare though with a group discount. We're done with competitions. The shelves in the office are overflowing with trophies now."

The Hot Flashes dancers got to work preparing a terrific hour-long show with all four groups participating. This was a freebie for the cruise line, but at least we would have the experience of performing on a cruise ship in our very own show.

It was a long and tiring journey on the day of departure. The troupe flew out of Tucson to Seattle at 6:00 a.m., changed planes to Anchorage, boarded a bus to Seward and arrived at the ship at 8:00 p.m. Dinner was served on board ship an hour later. It was after midnight when we finally curled up in bed.

It had been a rough day of travel for me from the start. At home I coped with a sinus problem which developed into a miserable cold and cough the morning we left Tucson. By evening I lost my voice completely and my ears were plugged. My roommate and I made a fine pair. When she removed her hearing aid, she could not hear and I could not talk.

Bright and early the next morning, I dragged myself out of bed to attend a tap workshop. The instructor taught us a complete routine in one hour, which I promptly forgot. But I took careful note of the words printed on her shirt which read, "Real Men Marry Dancers."

Way to go Paul! That must mean that the husbands of dancers have the stamina to withstand the stresses of their wives' passion for dance and hectic schedules.

During the tap workshop, the ship set sail toward the one-thousand mile inside- passage which would take us south to Vancouver, B.C. Canada, with several stops along the way. Although tour days while cruising were filled with tap classes and rehearsals, we could not avoid staring with awe at the magnificent mountains and dozens of long sinuous glaciers passing by.

To publicize the Hot Flashes' show, we slipped flyers under cabin doors and made announcements over the ship's intercom. We wanted the passengers to know the nightly Carnival shows were not the only entertainment onboard.

At last, it was time for our big show. Throughout the week I had rested as much of the time in the cabin as possible. My voice had returned and I was eager to take on this performance.

Jean led us out to "That's Entertainment", but when she took the mic, she showed the audience the professional emcee she was. She outdid herself with humor, timing, gusto and charm unsurpassed. Best of all, the place was packed in spite of the lunch hour. The Hot Flashes must have satisfied their appetites more than attractive lunch food.

From behind the curtains, I almost headed out on stage with a costume on backwards, but Lois and Carolyn stopped me just in time, and together they frantically turned the costume around. Since the ship was not in port, we had to cope with the swaying motion of the waves. Our reward for a grand performance under trying circumstances was a standing ovation which lasted endlessly, or so it seemed.

Wherever our dance troupe walked on the ship, people stopped us with praising comments like, "Wish you'd done two shows", "Far surpassed the Carnival entertainment", "Only show on this ship to receive a standing ovation", "I'm inspired to go home and try something similar" or "Your costumes are beautiful and dignified."

If the Carnival staff heard any of these statements they might have regretted printing a disclaimer in the Carnival Capers newsletter. On the day's schedule, it read "The Hot Flashes Tap Dance Group performs, 12:30 p.m. Atlantis Lounge." They should have stopped there, but they added, "Please note: This is not a Carnival Sponsored Event!!" Notice, not just one, but two exclamation marks. *Sorry Carnival, you can't take it back.*

The journey home was as lengthy as the trip up to Alaska had been.

Creeping behind a long slow line of vehicles crossing the border into Washington State and then coping with a four-hour airplane delay in Los Angeles, we did not arrive at Tucson airport until midnight. Paul, my "real man", was there to greet me at that late hour with a beautiful mixed bouquet of flowers. He is living proof that autumn is just as nice as spring; it is never too late to fall in love. We fell into bed at 1:30 a.m. What a day. What a week.

For the Hot Flashes, it was back to routine performances around town for the Beta Sigma Phi Regional Conference, Grandparents Day Fest, Doctors Breastfeeding Conference, Octoberfest, and Tucson High School's 55th Reunion. Each performance had its special qualities and challenges, but none to match the day we danced at the Casa Car Show.

Was there a dressing room at the car show? Not a one in sight. We did not even have a choice of dressing in a storeroom or outside behind a pillar, as at previous shows.

I wonder if celebrities ever have to face these types of conditions?

All that was left for us was to dress outside behind a tent, keeping our black leotards on as we changed costumes. But then a scary stage was the next obstacle facing us.

With assistance, we stepped up on milk crates to a high wooden stage to do the first number to "Boogie Woogie Bugle Boy."

My gosh! There is a drop off all the way around. One misstep and someone will be seriously injured. Now the stage is shaking, as I am. Hope it doesn't collapse.

We safely finished the dance and climbed down. What a relief when I heard Jean say, "We'll just go out and dance on the cement." The car show had advertised "cars, cars, cars", but as we ran out for each number, we had to slow down for "people, people, people" unaware that they were walking around on our stage. This was one show etched vividly in my memory. I can still see that stage swinging back and forth.

Channel 9 in Tucson presented a show titled "It Pays to be a Senior." The Hot Flashes were the seniors selected to demonstrate this theme. A camera man and an interviewer arrived at our dance studio to film the program. First they interviewed Jean. Next we staged a practice class with Jean instructing and correcting us. Then, dressed in our fringe costumes, we did our parade routine around the studio. Some of the dancers were interviewed and finally we performed "Stars and Stripes" in full costume.

I think the two fellows from Channel 9 enjoyed the entertainment. They probably rarely get that treat on their other assignments.

At the end of the year, it was once again time for the Fiesta Bowl parade in Phoenix. The Hot Flashes were welcomed back. Once a group has successfully made it through one parade, they are automatically enrolled again, if they wish. No auditions are necessary.

The dancers dressed in custom-made gold sparkly jackets with top hats, spats and shoes to match. White gloves completed the outfits. Of eighty-nine entrants, we were assigned number sixty-three, a big promotion from the year before. However, horses sandwiched us front and back.

I hope those pooper scoopers do their jobs.

One newspaper billed the parade as having a "Macy's Thanksgiving Day feel to it." We Hot Flashes did our part strutting and dancing down the avenue, tipping our hats to the spectators. I thought of that song, "If They Could See Me Now."

Feeling hot and sweaty with perspiration dripping down, in spite of temperatures in the 70s, we made it to the longer finish line at 3.5 miles. That year would be our second and final parade for the Fiesta Bowl. Too many of us experienced sore feet, legs and blisters. But the worse near-tragedy was when one of our dancers contracted a flesh-eating infection caused by a parasite bacteria entering through a non-healing blister on her foot. She was in the hospital for months and nearly died. She did recover, returned to the Hot Flashes and continued to be one of the group's best dancers.

"No more Fiesta Bowl parades," Jean emphasized. "Too long and too hard on the dancers. We showed them what we could do and that is enough. We'll stick to shorter performances from now on."

One afternoon after classes were over and the women had gone, Jean walked into the studio to find Bernie on a ladder putting up a dance poster of the Rockettes. If Bernie was not on a ladder, she might be making repairs on the roof or down in the bathrooms which required frequent plumbing repairs. She had earned the name of "Miss Fix-It", and every time something broke down in the ancient building, Jean yelled for Bernie.

This particular afternoon Jean was not after Bernie to solve a repair problem, she was on another mission. "Bernie, I have been thinking."

"Oh no, not another vision Jean."

Looking up at Bernie with pleading eyes, hoping for agreement, Jean stated, "We need to put on a show of our own."

Bernie finished applying the poster and climbed down the ladder. "Just where are we going to present this show? Here in the studio?"

"Oh, no, that's out of the question. How about the Gaslight Theater. We've performed there a few times during their intermissions."

"Jean, do you recall how small that stage is? Only twenty feet across. And they have no dressing rooms to speak of."

"We'll adjust by reducing the number of dancers for each number. I'm sure we can do it if they give their okay." Jean replied. "I'm going across the parking lot right now to see what they'll say."

CHAPTER FIFTEEN
GASLIGHT THEATER PRODUCTION

"These talented ladies are living proof that age doesn't mean slowing down." John Paul, *KCUN*

How do you stage your own show of thirty-four performers without a theater? If you are Jean Johnson, you find a way. The place chosen was the Gaslight Theater.

To the person in charge at the Gaslight, Jean made the request, "How about letting my Hot Flashes use your theater for one night? We've given you some freebies over here to fill in your intermissions, and we'd like to put on our own show for a change."

"Well, I guess we could give you a night when we have nothing else scheduled. But there is one stipulation. You will have to use our stage manager and lighting technician and pay their salaries for that evening."

The show was set for February 12, 2001 on a Monday at 6:00 p.m. Not the best time, but you take what you can get. For weeks the dance groups practiced on the theater stage instead of in the studio.

Everything was done first-class too. The studio spent two hundred dollars on the programs designed by Bernie, five hundred for a professional photographer to video the show, plus the wages for the stage manager and lighting technician. To help with expenses, members solicited ads from merchants in our shopping center to be placed in the program. Tickets were priced at $10 for general admission, $8 for seniors and $7 for ages twelve and under. All two-hundred sixty seats were sold out. People were calling the last day begging for tickets.

Dressing conditions presented a challenge. Some of the performers dressed in the narrow walkway back stage and others changed costumes behind enclosed curtains in the warm February air just outside the theater.

As the curtain rose slowly for this two-act performance, the audience first saw just the feet of the full cast squeezed onto this tiny stage, all tapping in rhythm to "42nd Street." Once the curtain reached its full height showing the owners of those feet, the introduction was over and they rushed off to make way for the first full number.

There were ten dances in each act with an additional presentation featuring Stacey, our choreographer, tapping to a song called "Swing." The enthusiastic audience applauded heartily at many parts of our dancing, not just with polite clapping at the end. Jean's witty and off-the-cuff comments between dances elicited lots of laughter too.

Following the finale and after flower bouquets were presented to Jean, Bernie and Stacey, Jean called out each of our names as we exited the stage down into the audience to shake their hands and thank them for coming. Our own show, another triumph, took the cast of the Hot Flashes to the top of that mountain once more.

After the big show, one might think we were tapped out. Oh, no! The following night the Hot Flashes danced for the Chaparral Business Women's Group at the Viscount Hotel.

I am so glad to see a wooden stage instead of that carpeted one on which we did an entire show here so long ago.

About thirty women were seated at a long table which was off center from the stage. As we shifted to stage right while dancing, we found ourselves looking out and smiling at the wall where there were no spectators. It's a good thing that dance sometimes recaptures the freedom of child's play. You need to have discipline, but also have fun and the ability to laugh at yourself.

Imagining faces smiling back at me helps a lot.

At the completion of the show, the ladies at the back of the table stood and applauded, while the ones in front stayed seated, unaware that the ones behind them were standing. Guess that could be called a half-standing ovation.

The following month Jean received an invitation to provide entertainment outdoors in downtown Tucson for the Governor's Employee Awareness Celebration. Our stage was not on the sidewalk, not on a raised stage above the street, but on the street itself, one that had big gaps in it.

From the dressing room in a building overlooking the street below, the dancers hurried down outside stairs to the sidewalk and out to the street before posing in place until the music began.

As we danced, we put on our biggest smiles and tried not to be distracted by the loud mariachi band down the street and the camera man moving among us taking close-ups of our faces. There is a country western song that says, "Dance like nobody's watching." In our case, that included like nobody is filming. Of course, the performers kept an eye out for those holes in the street. Luckily no one twisted or broke an ankle.

The government workers watching in the street, from the sidewalk and on the stairs, were very pleased with our performance. We received a letter of appreciation several days later. Excerpts from the chairperson of the Governor's Employee Awareness Celebration Committee read, "Our survey tells us you were the hit of our event. Now you are the talk of the state complex. You all deserve a pat on the back for a job well done."

Compliments, praises and awards, though always hard-earned and welcomed, did not stop Jean from putting on her visionary glasses to see where else she could take the Hot Flashes. Occasionally, a new member suggested what she thought was a new idea to improve the dance troupe only to hear Jean respond, "Been there, done that."

However, there was one suggestion Jean had not tried. It came from several long-time members of Group Three. "Jean, what do you think of having a comedy dance, a really funny skit? One tap dance following another is fine for a while, but wouldn't it be better to insert some comic relief? Just listen to our idea." Jean listened, gave her approval and that is how the "Mop Ladies" were born.

Figure 25 The "Mop Ladies"

They were a hit from the start. Dressed as cleaning ladies, they entered carrying buckets, mops and brooms and proceeded to scrub the stage while tapping to the song "That's Life." The sketch drew laughter throughout the dance. One high achiever in their midst attempted to follow the tap steps of the others, but continuously failed. The laughter reached its highest pitch when Pat popped balloons, one at a time, which were hidden at her bust under her bib overalls. That act was a winner at every show.

In fairness to the other dance groups in the Hot Flashes, humor was also included in some of their novelty dances such as "Splish Splash", "Jail House Rock" and "Sadie Hawkins".

During 2001, the bookings kept coming, accompanied by successes, challenges and embarrassments. Performing for the Soroptimist fashion show proved to be full of obstacles. On a large raised T-shaped stage with a ramp extended into the audience, we performed "Boogie Woogie." At the end of the dance, we moved back, posed and smiled at the audience for two minutes while the fashion show was in progress. Believe me, two minutes is a long time to hold a smile. A break in the fashion parade gave us time to do our "Stars and Stripes" number, then strut off the stage to "That's Entertainment." The show was over for the Hot Flashes.

The dancers met more challenges at St. Demetrius Hellenic Community Center. They were not well prepared for us, to put it mildly. First, we stood outside for half an hour while the organizers searched for a dressing room. Next, we waited for them to finish serving and eating dinner. Third, we ended up outside in the night air dancing on a brick surface in dim lighting. Since the space was too small inside the building, the audience moved outside after eating.

Our music had to be piped through speakers to the outside. That took time to set up as we stood there shifting from one foot to the other. Finally, we lined up for "Boogie Woogie", but the music did not start. While we waited for them to correct the problem, Jean captured the audience's attention with her famous introduction, "We are the award winning Hot Flashes! We don't dust, we don't iron, we don't cook; all we ever do is dance."

After she introduced us, she tried her well-worn joke about being born during the war, and the North was winning. Paul had given her other jokes, but she could not recall them. But with her skill at adlibbing, she amused the audience with witty anecdotes.

Once they fixed that fifth and final problem, at last we could dance. The show was about as perfect as it could be, in spite of talkers and other distractions from the younger crowd. We demonstrated great precision. Practice makes perfect, but does patience also make perfect?

Obstacles continued to plague our performances, but at least they made us a stronger and more cohesive team. Besides, the problems encountered were good conversation topics, often related to others with embellishments.

The new Desert Diamond Casino, just south of Tucson, invited us to entertain for a special show, "A Diamond American Tribute." The Hot Flashes and Big Band Express headlined the program which was wildly advertised on radio, in newspapers and through the distribution of flyers.

The stage was set up in their outdoor plaza and we were scheduled to perform at 3:00 p.m. There was no dressing room, so the dancers changed at the side of a building, completely exposed but far enough away from the audience not to be noticed.

Oh, I see there is a table and chairs. I'll crouch down behind them.

During the performance the sun beat down and sometimes directly into our eyes. Even though it was late October, the temperature was around 90 degrees. A huge crowd arrived. Some bore the heat in chairs set up in the direct sun, while others hovered in the shade of the buildings.

Strong wind gusts occurred throughout the show, but thankfully slowed down during "Business of Love", a number where we sat on stools, danced around them and kicked our legs over the stools. Two of the dancers did not raise their legs high enough and knocked their stools over. A quick-thinking man in the audience, with Jean's permission, sneaked in among us and set those stools back up. Saved by a spectator.

Figure 26 Group 1 posing for "Business of Love", a jazz dance

By the conclusion of the show, the crowd had nearly doubled. Praises galore were showered on us, but one compliment in particular stood out. A man, using his cellphone, had called his wife during the show and told her, "You won't believe this group of fantastic dancers I'm watching. You need to get right over here."

That pumped us up as we floated back and down to the exposed outdoor dressing area. Then reality sank in. Although the Hot Flashes were special out there to an adoring crowd, behind the scenes, we were ordinary modest ladies hiding and covering ourselves up as we rushed to dress and go home.

Six weeks later found the troupe at the old original Desert Diamond to dance indoors for the Bingo players. This time we were treated to a curtained indoor dressing section just behind the stage. I wondered if the players might begrudge us holding up their Bingo games with our show. Not at all. Their smiles and tremendous applause indicated otherwise. One woman hollered out, "You make me proud to me a woman."

I wonder if she would have made that same statement if she had seen our other show.

At a different show, as a group of dancers entered the stage, they wiped their shoes on paper towels covered with rosin to keep from slipping. However, the paper towels stuck to the soles of some of the tap shoes throughout the routine. Pat, one of the dancers, related later how she put on a happy face on the outside, but was belly laughing on the inside watching the others struggling to shuffle and flap.

I hope they didn't have to do buffaloes, where one foot crossed up over the other giving more exposure to those paper towels.

If that wasn't enough for one night, one of the dancer's jackets came open during "Stars and Stripes", exposing her bra. She was one to laugh at herself, so no doubt back stage she probably said something like, "At least I had a bra on."

By now we were charging $150 for a half-hour show, but Jean usually gave them forty minutes of stage time. An hour performance was $300, which did not slow down the bookings. The Hot Flashes stopped doing malls because there were too many distractions and not many donations deposited into our tip jar.

However, when we received a call from Dan at KSAZ begging us to perform at the Park Mall on a Friday at 11:00 a.m., Jean could not refuse. We left our suitcases in a locked conference room and carried some of our costumes and props through the long passages for authorized personnel only to reach the center court. Spectators filled most of the chairs set up for their convenience. Others took time out from their shopping to stand and watch the show.

I must admit I enjoyed performing in that mall despite the loud noises and movement of people passing by. I put a tremendous amount of energy into the show, but I think I reaped twice as much exercise walking back and forth on slippery cement through the long secret passage to retrieve some of my costumes from the conference room.

Jean's health continued to deteriorate. Besides breathing difficulties, she had to deal with back and knee problems. More often than not she asked one of our dancers to substitute as emcee at performances. Some days she was not well enough to go to the studio, but even in her absence an instructor was present to conduct classes. Bernie made frequent visits to the studio to report on Jean's health, make tapes for the routines and attend to the never-ending repairs.

Streams of requests for shows continued to pour in, which Bernie took from their home. She and Jean made certain we always kept our commitments. If they took a booking, the Hot Flashes reliably showed up ready to dance.

So the performances continued with their ups and downs. Speaking of downs, there were several of those at the seventh annual fund-raising Shriners show. Julie, one of our dancers, slipped and hit the floor with a wham just before entering the stage. Another dancer, Bonnie, tripped and fell in the dressing room pulling Mary Wells down with her. Another Mary suffered a mild heart attack before going on for her dance. Paramedics came and took her to the hospital. She recovered quickly. The other fall victims performed their dances as usual. Notice that no falls occurred on stage. Perhaps that is why we were told it was the "best show ever."

By the year 2002 the Hot Flashes could call themselves parade veterans. We had danced and marched year after year in nearly every parade that came along like the Copper Bowl, St. Patrick's Day, Fiesta Bowl and Veteran's Day. We were invited to "saddle up" for the 51st Rex Allen Days parade to be held in Wilcox, Arizona, eighty miles east of Tucson. So off we galloped, by car of course, to help celebrate a tribute to Rex Allen, a former singing cowboy of television and movies.

This was a huge parade for a small country town. We were number fifteen of ninety entries. Carole Kirshner, one of our Hot Flashes, stayed ahead of the dance group and signaled instructions with her baton. We danced nearly the entire mile in the warm and sunny October morning. The best part was to see Jean up ahead, strong enough to walk the entire route, guiding us through seven blocks of downtown Wilcox.

Afterwards, the judges announced, "For the Best Marching Group, this award goes to the Hot Flashes." They handed the trophy to a beaming Jean Johnson. She had much to be proud about; she brought the Hot Flashes a long way.

Figure 27 Charlie decorating the van for the Veteran's Day parade

Figure 28 The Hot Flashes marching in the Veteran's Day parade (Husband, Paul, following beside them)

Figure 29 In front of the reviewing stand

In the months that followed, we continued to progress. KGUN-TV sent an announcer and a cameraman to present a live broadcast from our Broadway studio. Beginning at 5:30 a.m., everything moved like clockwork because Bernie had posted the exact time for each group to perform. During our dances the announcer communicated from the studio with a woman anchor at the station, trading complimentary comments about our dancing techniques.

It is so distracting with the cameraman moving among us and pulling that cord around. Hope I don't trip over it. It's an interesting experience, but I'd rather do a live performance on the stage anytime.

In the middle of summer a group of dancers flew to "the city of indulgence" Las Vegas to compete in the North American Dance Competition.

I had thought and hoped that we had given up those expensive and tiresome competitions.

The Hot Flashes did get six gold medals out of that national competition, which gave Jean more bragging material for all our shows which followed.

The reign of the Hot Flashes was not over yet. Not only had we been publicized in *Dance Teacher Now* magazine, but we also appeared in *Family Circle* and *US World and News Report*. We were determined to maintain the reputation of the Hot Flashes as a first-class dance troupe. Three major events were on the horizon such as the Hot Flashes had never experienced in their years together.

CHAPTER SIXTEEN
TUSON'S FOX THEATER

"Hot Flashes send chills to the audience with their energy and vitality." Lupito Murillo

A group of Arizona business people had a vision. They imagined the seventy-two year old Fox Theater in downtown Tucson restored to its former glory. That old movie theater had been closed and stood dormant for longer than they could remember. It would take a fortune to replace those raggedy seats, glass chandeliers, broken stage and the peeling walls. It looked frozen in time, as though one night after the final movie reel had ended, the audience walked back up the aisles, the manager turned off the lights, locked up the theater and never looked back.

But now folks were wanting those good old days again. "We want to see family movies, stage plays and live entertainment," they lamented. So that group of visionary people who first planted the idea in the community went to work raising thousands of dollars so that gradually the Fox began to look like its former self. To keep people interested and to demonstrate progress, it was decided to stage a ceremony to light the recreated sign and marque, even though the interior was not complete.

The Hot Flashes were asked to perform as the featured entertainment. An uneven raised wooden stage was set up across the middle of the street near the theater. The dancers dressed inside the closed theater. On a warm but windy June evening, we wound our way through 200 standing spectators applauding us even before we walked up on the stage. Posing and smiling, of course, and ready to begin the first dance, we stood terminally long to hear the first notes of our music.

What is going wrong? This wind is keeping me off balance. Always some technical problem. Sure enough, someone had unplugged the cord.

Finally, we heard the familiar beginning notes of "42nd Street", and our program was off and running. As each group took its turn, the darkening night sky and the brightly colored lights focusing on the dancers enhanced the overall effect. At the conclusion of our program, we stepped down from the stage through prolonged applause to be met by Mayor Walkup who shook hands with each of us.

Once the sky was completely dark, the moment for which the crowd was waiting arrived. The sign and the marque, containing more than 150 bulbs and about 187 feet of neon tubes, sent off a spectacular light into the darkness. The crowd oohed and awed and cried out, "Beautiful!" The Fox Theater lives again.

Dancing along with the Hot Flashes through the years, memorable moments continued to build. At one location, disaster struck when toilets overflowed into our dressing room. "Mop Ladies" where were you when we needed you? At another venue, the metal strips connecting the sections of a raised stage started coming apart as we were dancing. Two men managed to reconnect the sections so at least none of us fell through the gap for the rest of the program.

One difficult challenge occurred at the La Paloma Resort where a two-day event was held to honor former Notre Dame Coach, Ara Parseghian. Golf and tennis tournaments, a gala dinner, a silent auction and a performance by Pam Tillis were included in the price at $1000 per person. Proceeds went to Ara Parseghian Medical Research Foundation to find a cure for Neiman-Pick Type C disease. Three of Ara's grandchildren had been afflicted and two had died.

After the gala dinner, the Hot Flashes performance was the surprise for Ara's 80th birthday. Group Four carried in two cakes with two lit candles on each. The rest of us followed with our tambourine parade routine while singing "Happy Birthday".

Some problems arose when dancing on carpet, tripping on wires and dividers and not seeing the audience. Most of the 1,000 spectators were watching us on large video screens, but they really cheered us on. Ara exclaimed, "I didn't know they flew in the Rockettes from New York."

For another show, we introduced a new dance, "Be Our Guest." Dressed as French waitresses, in black and white costumes and wearing white bows tied in back, we carried in pizza pans on raised hands. After twirling around and doing a number of tricky maneuvers with those pans, we set them down and tap danced upon them. The audience loved that dance.

I am so relieved that not one of us dropped our pans as we did in rehearsal.

Figure 30 Dancers ready to serve for "Be Our Guest"

The Fox Theater was the first of three major events coming our way. The second was about to top even that.

CHAPTER SEVENTEEN
JERRY LEWIS TELETHON

"A dozen pair of gams doing the heel toe shuffle like there's no tomorrow!" Bonnie Henry, *Arizona Daily Star*

"Stay up late or get up early for Hot Flashes" the newspaper headlines read. If folks wanted to watch the Hot Flashes perform live at 3:30 a.m. on the 38th Jerry Lewis Muscular Dystrophy Research Telethon, they needed to stay up way past their bedtimes or set their alarms.

"It was one of my dreams for the group to be nationally recognized, and this is an excellent cause," Jean told the newspapers. She then related the Hot Flashes' past achievements which included the state and nationally televised commercials, the Fiesta Bowl, the Gaslight Theater and many holiday parades.

Telethon organizers heard about us when they conducted a "Stars Across America" search for singers, dancers, bands, comedian, and novelty acts. Out of thousands, fifteen acts were chosen. They either spotted the Hot Flashes on our unique website or from a video sent in by Bernie. In either case, we were one of the lucky ones to be selected.

In the studio Jean had more to tell us. "Say, you will be sharing the stage with other celebrities such as Cher and Celine Dion, but not at the same time of course. The time slot is certainly not desirable, but I figured we're happy to even be called. Besides, we can't look a gift horse in the mouth. The flight, hotel and meals are all paid for. At last we are finally making it to Hollywood."

Sadly Jean, whose dream was to participate in the telethon, was not able to attend because of illness. She sent Bernie to accompany and take charge of Group One and Two, sixteen dancers in all, as we boarded our flight to Los Angeles.

Two drivers met us at the airport and drove us to the Hollywood Beverly Hilton Hotel. A picture of Merv Griffin, owner of the Hilton's 'Home of the Stars', welcomed guests with a statement telling us that every president since John F. Kennedy had stayed there.

At lunch we shared the dining room with other entertainers. Among them, Charo, a pretty bubbly lady who once sang with Xavier Cugat's orchestra, chatted with us and even had her picture taken with us. She stirred up a little friendly competition with the Dancing Dads at a nearby table when she told us that they said they were better dancers than us. It was not true they said that, but we stood up and executed a perfect times step and the Dancing Dads showed off their times step. I know we outshined them.

At seven o'clock that evening a limo service drove our troupe to CBS Studios for a dress rehearsal. After we were given directions on exactly what to expect when it was time to do the live performance, they permitted us to run through our numbers on the stage.

I am impressed with the polite and respectful treatment we are given.

The next day, Sunday, we were on our own. Some of the ladies shared a taxi to Grauman's Chinese Theater. The theater was closed, but we enjoyed looking at the handprints embedded in cement in front of the theater. These famous stars from yesteryear not only left their handprints but added a few words to remember them by. They were my heroes and I aspired to be just like them.

Back at the hotel, we found a place to rehearse our routines in a turf-covered courtyard. Although we could not use our taps, just going through the movements built up confidence for the upcoming telethon performance.

Everybody is so excited.

That night we did not retire until ten o'clock to catch a couple of hours of sleep, in hopes of resting up for our 3:30 a.m. performance. I didn't sleep a wink.

Up at midnight, we applied our stage makeup and met in the lobby to await the limo service. Arriving at the CBS television studio at 1:45 a.m., we were greeted by a man who escorted us to a dressing room. One by one, we were called into another room for touch-ups on makeup and hair. One last transfer took us into a room in which we could sit and view the show in progress on a television screen and partake of sandwiches and drinks.

None of us are eating any of that tasty food. Not before going on stage.

At last, the big moment arrived. The Hot Flashes were taken to the stage to wait behind the curtain. Each of our groups was to do one dance. The emcee introduced us by saying, "No rocking chairs or Bingo for these fabulous ladies."

The signal was given and out danced Group Two to perform "All That Jazz." No sooner did they finish and run off the stage, Group One moved out as we had been instructed. We posed, the music began for "Happy Feet" and we were tapping away. What a surprise to see an audience at that hour in the morning filling every seat in the studio, cheering and applauding our performances.

What a thrill to be on national television. I am so wide awake and enjoying every minute of this. I don't want it to end.

Once the dance finished we were instructed to stay on the stage. Group Two was called back to join us. The emcee praised the precision, the smiles, the costumes and the energy put into our dances while we stood there soaking up every complimentary word. The audience burst out laughing when he said, "Their video will be coming out soon called 'Really Mature Women Gone Wild!'"

Back at the hotel, we gathered in one of the member's rooms to watch ourselves on the television screen. That was possible because the show had been delayed one hour in the three Pacific states. I think each dancer was pleased, judging by the smiles I saw on their faces as they finished viewing themselves on the TV. The camera had moved around, giving close-ups of each dancer. It really showed us off.

At our early morning breakfast we were wide-eyed, talkative and still feeling the excitement of performance. But the lack of sleep from being up all night was beginning to take its effect.

By the time the dance teams boarded the plane for Tucson, we were hollow-eyed and weary-worn. The sleepy Hot Flashes were probably the quietest passengers on the flight for once. Each, no doubt, was snoozing and dreaming of those special moments on the telethon stage.

We did not see Jerry Lewis in person in Hollywood because he appeared on the telethon from another city. We did receive the following letter of appreciation from him, with copies to Clint Eastwood, Julia Roberts, Tom Cruise, Tony Orlando and Max Alexander.

AUGUST 31, 2003

DEAR !

WEBSTER: "FRIEND"... ONE WHO
HOLDS A PERSONAL REGARD FOR
ANOTHER.

I THANK YOU FOR THAT REGARD.

ALWAYS,

JERRY

CC: CLINT EASTWOOD, JULIA ROBERTS,
TOM CRUISE, TONY ORLANDO,
MAX ALEXANDER

Figure 31 Jerry Lewis' letter to the Hot Flashes

You may ask who would arise at three thirty in the morning to watch the Hot Flashes perform live on the telethon. My loyal neighbor did and from then on she repeated that tale to anyone she could corral to listen to her.

That year the Jerry Lewis Telethon raised a record $60.5 million, with Tucsonans pledging $441,825 of that amount. It was a great experience for the Hot Flashes dancers. More than just performing on national television, we played a small part in aiding a worthy cause.

From the world of stardom on the national stage, we returned to other ordinary stages with their successes, flaws, joys and foul-ups. At the Alzheimer's Association Memory Walk, we presented an overall satisfying show, except when the elastic band on my cowgirl hat broke just before entering the stage to do "Favorite Son". Throughout the dance, the dangling strap could not keep my hat from rocking back and forth. Somehow that hat stayed on when we jumped up from our stools to move out to perform. Those energetic trenches caused my hat to wobble even more.

Oh, I am glad that dance is over.

Figure 32 Doing the trenches in "Favorite Son"

Back stage one of the dancers had her own problems as she struggled to put on her costume. Tugging and pulling, she could not stretch that costume to fit her heavy-set body. She began to cry, thinking that she had gained weight. She was mistaken. Her costume, in that crowded room, had been mixed-up with the costume of a petite dancer who might have thought she lost weight. With relief, they exchanged outfits and were ready to run out to the stage.

My favorite of all the dances I ever learned was "Be My Guest" accompanied by the music from the musical "Beauty and the Beast." But dancing with pizza pans could be a bit tricky at times. Twice I pulled some blunders. At the 200+ Dance Festival, when taking a bow, I knocked Jane's pizza pan out of her hand, causing a loud clatter. Not a good way to end a dance.

Worse yet, was the time I forgot to bring my pizza pan to Manor at Midvale. It was too far from home to drive back to retrieve it. What to do? The kitchen did not have pizza pans, but three of our dancers put their heads together and solved the problem. Judy Richey presented the idea, Carole Kershner contributed her large round hat box lid, and Helen Francisco suggested covering the lid with foil borrowed from the kitchen. Voila, an appropriate word to use, to match the French singer in our song. I now had a very stylish pizza pan. Do not worry, I did not dance on it, but behind it, so I should not crush the hat box lid. Anyway, it worked and I was forever grateful to those creative dancers.

The third major event was about to happen. Jean took the call. "An invitation? When? Let me write this down. October 29th at 9:00 a.m. Where did you say" Oh, okay, in front of Centennial Hall. Yes, yes, you can count on us. We will be there."

"Bernie, everybody, anybody, the entire city of Tucson," Jean yelled. "The 42nd Street" cast from New York is coming to town and wants to meet and dance with the Hot Flashes!".

CHAPTER EIGHTEEN
DANCING WITH THE 42ND STREET CAST

"Take risks, act on your dreams, become the stars you were meant to be."

What a day! What great memories! It was a beautiful, sunny cool morning when the Hot Flashes hurried down to greet part of the New York cast from the "42nd Street" professional production. A small raised stage was set up in front of the Centennial Hall Theater on the University of Arizona campus. We could not have asked for a better setting, a low green hedge at the back of the stage with towering palm trees beyond.

Before long, seven men and women from the "42nd Street" cast walked out of the theater to greet us. Jean introduced herself and started the program by telling them, "It's an honor to be here with you. We know we'll be inspired by your example, and we feel privileged to demonstrate what women three times your age can accomplish through hours of practice, persistence and hard work."

Since this event had not been advertised, the audience was small, consisting mostly of husbands and friends. College students walking by stopped a while, curious to see what was happening.

The dancers from the professional production cast wore practice clothes, black tank tops with red "42nd Street" letters across the front. In contrast, the Hot Flashes wore costumes and stage makeup as we always do for performances. Our costume change place was in the ladies restroom inside the theater.

The Hot Flashes and the "42nd Street" cast alternated dance numbers. They did a routine, then we showed them what we could do. Watching their energy, hearing their clear taps and seeing their smiles made me stand there in awe.

Oh, to be young again and to be like them.

The Hot Flashes performed three dances, and then it was time for our rendition of "42nd Street". Seven of us ladies ran up on that stage, posed in our pretty pink costumes with matching bows on our shoes, ready for the music to start.

Can we come anywhere near their level? What will they think when they see us doing steps that we borrowed from their dance? I must not make a mistake. I'll give it everything I've got. We may be a tad slower than those "42nd Street" dancers, but we'll show them how capable we are.

Figure 33 "42nd Street" - They danced

Did we ever show them! I think they were surprised at our abilities. Comments overheard from the cast as we danced included, "Amazing" "Take a look at that step" and "Unbelievable!" Jane, one of our original dancers, started referring to the Hot Flashes as "talent on tap."

136

Figure 34 "42nd Street" - We danced

At the conclusion of the program, we did a times step, and then the "42nd Street" cast showed us one of theirs. Two television stations taped the performances and interviewed Jean and some of the "42nd Street" cast. We mingled and individually met with the performers in the same area where we had danced. They were all so friendly and showered us with compliments. One of the dancers told us, "Meeting with a local tap group was a first for us."

When we asked another young woman from the cast what part she performed in the show, she replied, "I'm a swing. I fill in for any one of twenty-two dancers on the spur of the moment." In other words, she had to know everyone's part.

I can't even imagine it for myself. It's all I can do to learn my own part. Occasionally one of the Hot Flash dancers had to take another dancer's part, but we usually knew a day ahead and had a chance to practice it.

Before we parted company, the "42nd Street" cast presented each of us with tickets to the show that night. In addition, they gave each of us a little mirror as a memento. The silver cover was engraved with "42nd Street, Best Musical" and at the bottom were the words, "You're going out there a youngster…" Then, as you open the cover to look at the mirror, there is a picture of a star underlined by the words, "…but you've got to come back a star."

We certainly were not youngsters when we joined the Hot Flashes, but like children we were curious and open to new things. We expressed hope, enthusiasm and excitement, no matter our years. Each dancer, in her own right, eventually did become a star. So every time I used that mirror, I could be reminded of how far I had come.

That evening following the award-winning "42nd Street" show, we Hot Flashes waited at the stage door to see those performers we danced with that morning. Finally, out the door they appeared. We shouted, "Congratulations", hugged them and wished them continuing successful careers. Another memorable day in the lives of the Hot Flashes.

Jean's health continued to deteriorate. We began to see less of her during the following months. Many days she could not even make it to the studio. At our performances, assigned dancers frequently filled in for her as emcee. We wondered how much longer we could carry on without her. Her foresight and her energy were the driving forces of our organization.

There were still numerous shows on the books and many groups counting on us for their entertainment. We forged ahead because we loved dancing, performing at the Berger Arts Center Theater, entertaining for the Eastside Seniors at the Hilton Hotel and putting on a winter Christmas show for the Sun City Singles Club.

The University of Arizona Women's Basketball team wanted us back once more for their half-time entertainment at a two-day tournament. We performed a routine to the music "Waltz Me" dressed in western gear. A requirement this time was no taps on their newly finished basketball court floor. We adapted by wearing white sneakers. But even without the tapping sound, we all seemed to have found pleasure performing for 1700 people in attendance the first day and 1200 more basketball fans on the second day.

Most of our performances were successful, but there were some we would just have soon forgotten. In some shows we made lots of mistakes. Jean's favorite criticism was that we "looked like a can of worms". On rare occasions folks sitting in the front row slept during the entire performance. That's show business.

One afternoon I received a call from Bernie. "Did you see today's paper? The Women's Foundation of Southern Arizona want to honor local women for their fifth annual Tribute Book. The *Arizona Daily Star* will devote two pages in their Accent section to women who are honored for what they've accomplished. Don't you think Jean would qualify?"

"Absolutely," I replied.

"Claire, how about you nominating her? You have to write an essay of no more than 500 words of why she should be selected. This would be a great thing to do for Jean. Are you willing?"

"I suppose. I don't know if I could do her justice, but I will give it a shot."

Bernie called Mary Wells, one of our dancers and a good writer, to make the same request. Both of us heeded Bernie, and sent in the letters to nominate Jean. An excerpt from our essays made the *Tucson Arizona Star*. A number of other women were acknowledged in the paper, but only a selected few were honored in large print accompanied by a photo. Jean was one of them. A condensed version of our essays related how she established the Hot Flashes and told how they have performed for hundreds of audiences. Jean's story was placed in the Tribute Keepsake Book entitled "In Celebration of Women Everyday Heroes."

The Hot Flashes continued to be game for anything as long as it included dancing or photo sessions. A relative of one of our members invited us to her horse ranch to have pictures taken. Changing into three different costumes in her house, we tramped around outside through the dirt in our tap shoes to locate various backdrops for our photos. We posed in a bright green "We're in the Money" costume with the pasture behind us. We surrounded the thick branches of a mesquite tree wearing our "Favorite Son" turquoise and white costumes. In our pure white "Sing, Sing, Sing" costumes, we posed in two places, alongside a corral fence and by an open-air horse-drawn carriage with a couple of our dancers sitting inside the old buggy. Missing from the picture was the horse, of course, but we somehow could not corral any horses that day to pose with us. They had more important plans, I suspect, such as looking for greener pastures.

Jean occasionally had her 'feel good' days and was up to giving her grand introduction for the Hot Flashes and filling in the empty stage time with witty anecdotes while we changed. In January of 2004, she made it to the two-day Dance Festival. The *Aztec Press* wrote "The Hot Flashes tap dancing act, without doubt, stole the show." Five days later Jean was on the mic at the Gay Nineties program honoring folks over ninety years old at The Fountains retirement home.

It's just like old times. She appears to have made a complete recovery.

The passion to perfect our dances showed up in our willingness to practice, not only several days during the week, but even on Saturday mornings. A few of us let ourselves into the empty studio at seven o'clock to work on new dances and to review the older ones. Anytime, anywhere, even waiting in grocery lines the feet moved to a particular tap step. Some dancers awoke during the night visualizing routines, especially if there was to be a show the next day. We were as devoted to dance as Olympic athletes are to their sports.

By this time the Hot Flashes were considered semi-professional, mainly because of their precision and the other demands Jean placed on the dancers. Learning to dance required a watchful eye on the instructor, a good ear attuned to the beat of the music and a sharp mind to focus not only on the present step but on the steps to follow.

However, no matter how many classes we had and how often we practiced, we needed an appreciative audience to reward us. Requests for the Hot Flashes continued to pour in.

Our favorite venues were the ones with the large stages, so that all our dancers could be included. Besides, the larger number of dancers, the greater the impact on the audience. Additionally, now that we danced with the large pizza pans, we utilized a wider space to avoid collisions and prevent pans from flying.

One warm and windy afternoon in April, Santa Catalina Villas, a lovely retirement home in the foothills, welcomed the Hot Flashes and promised the residents in their newsletter "a tapping smashing performance", but for us it was far from smashing.

A wide but shallow wooden floor stage was placed on a grassy, slightly inclined slope facing a swimming pool. The audience sat across the pool.

That's no good. They are too remote. They'll lose interest in us.

To add to the placement problem, no microphone had been provided for Jean so she had to shout to make her voice heard above the wind. To top that off, the weak sound system could not project a loud enough music sound for that far-away audience. During "Be My Guest", we waitresses almost lost our pizza trays to the gusty winds. If we had, they would have looked like flying saucers off in space.

Now that would have grabbed the attention of those folks across the pool who appeared to have lost interest in the show and were talking among themselves.

On days when Jean had recovered from a bout of her chronic breathing difficulties, she came into the studio to check on our progress and to give us news of upcoming engagements. All very pleasant and positive information until she frequently asked, "Anyone want to buy the Hot

Flashes?"

Oh, how I dreaded that question. I don't ever want you to sell it. I want to be a Hot Flashes tap dancer till I can't lift a foot off the ground.

In October of that year, the Shadow Mountain Country Club, formerly known as Sunsites Community Center at Pierce, Arizona, requested the Hot Flashes for a third time. We hired a bus and driver to take us on the 90-mile trip.

We Hot Flashes really go in style.

It was a pleasure to dance on their new staging area. We old-timers recalled a terrible night ten years before when one of our dancers slipped and fell in the former location and broke her wrist, ending her dancing career. Bernie scattered tons of rosin on this new tiled floor and no one slipped. Dressing rooms in this building were still not adequate. Some dancers dressed in the men's bathroom and others in the ladies room, the kitchen and the office.

While waiting to go on, I began to daydream. *My ideal dressing room is one large enough to hold all the dancers with enough space to keep from mixing up costumes. No more crying over costumes that somehow mysteriously had shrunk. Add mirrors, tables, chairs and pitchers of water. Better yet, give us a dressing room close to the stage.*

How many times have we run back the long stretch to a distant dressing room, out of breath from the last dance, while pulling off hats and gloves as we go along? Once inside, we yank off our costumes, squeeze into the next, begging someone to zip up our backs. One last look in the mirror to see if hats are on straight, then run back through grass, dirt and gravel, still pulling on gloves. Hearing the emcee announcing us, we dash on stage, take over positions, smile and all the while gasping for breath. Somehow, I can't imagine those famous tap dancers like Ginger Rogers, Eleanor Powell and Ann Miller having to endure all that.

"It's time you're on", I hear Bernie awakening me from my reverie. So off I went to join my group to put on our dance, but this time I'm not out of breath.

Jean could not make the long trip to Pierce, Arizona, so Gloria Jean, who had recently joined Group Two, assumed the duties of emcee and did an excellent job. Our performance went well considering we entertained at a late hour just the night before.

Afterward we enjoyed dinner together at a nearby restaurant. On the return bus ride, we watched a video of the show we had just completed and cheered and applauded each other's performances.

The art of tap appeals to so many people. Although it is not as popular as it was back in the 1920s and 1930s, there is something about the syncopated sounds of tap that causes all ages to sit up and listen. As we were leaving after one of our performances, a man hurried across the parking lot to say, "What a cute group you are. I didn't know it was a tap group. I couldn't tear myself away." May this particular American art form always have this effect on audiences. Long live tap dancing.

Jean's last time as emcee was on October 15, 2004 at the Hilton Hotel. Speaking to retirees of the USS Bryer, she did her usual opening talk once the music that brought us on the stage had stopped. "We are the award-winning Hot Flashes. We have performed in New York, Hollywood and in fund-raisers such as the Jerry Lewis Telethon, marched and tapped in the Fiesta Bowl parade and won many trophies in competition. We've danced on cement, grass, wet stages, cloth, gravel and plastic, but we do whatever it takes to put on a great show." After hearing that build-up, we did our best to present the promised great show to the reunion of Navy retirees.

Figure 35 Jean's last time as emcee

Backstage at the conclusion of the program, Jean told us, "It was a wonderful show. I am so proud of my Hot Flashes." Perhaps she knew that this was to be her last show. We certainly did not know. Some may have suspected her frailty, while others like me may have refused to believe the warning signs.

We struggled on without Jean through three more performances. Our last show was on November 11, 2004 at the Hilton Hotel for representatives of military organizations from all over the United States. All four of our groups put on an outstanding show.

What a way to go out.

For thirteen years the Hot Flashes brought on many smiles as they tapped their way into the hearts of the folks who watched them. But it was over. As the weeks went by Jean became weaker as her illness gradually took its toll. In the end, she decided not to sell the Hot Flashes. She was afraid in the hands of someone else that the group would lose its special qualities and fail. She wanted people to remember the high standards and exemplary performances of the Hot Flashes.

Jean died on February 9, 2005. Before she left she told her dear companion, Bernie, "You were the wind beneath my wings." How very true. Although Jean possessed the vision, the tap experience and the knowledge to organize and inspire, Bernie balanced her perfectly with her technical skills. Together they made the Hot Flashes a success.

Jean Johnson will not be forgotten. Her name is memorialized on several tiles in the "Women's Plaza of Honor" on the University of Arizona campus. As Sherry Young, one of the Hot Flash dancers, wrote after Jean's death, "Jean Johnson was a woman with a vision to make life more fun and more interesting for senior women and to bring entertainment and joy to others. She will be remembered for her wit, her compassion and her conviction that we senior women could do anything she imagined for us."

Dear Jean, you were right. Everyone who entered through your Tucson studio doors had their lives changed, just as you promised. Experienced dancers and those who gave it a try for the first time, took lessons and tried out the stage. Even for those who did not stay, their lives changed too. Perhaps they found the commitment to dance was not for them, but they now had the courage to try other new endeavors.

Each of us played a role, but without your vision and determination, dear Jean, there would never have been a Hot Flashes. You gave us courage and dignity. "Who could believe a hot flash could change a life?" as you liked to say. We believed it. Thank you Jean.

From that well-known song the Hot Flashes sang to our audiences at the end of a performance, it is time to say to Jean, Bernie and the Hot Flashes, "We'll meet again, don't know where, and we don't know when, but I know we'll meet again some sunny day."

LETTERS AND POEMS

Letter Following Jean's Death

I can't tell you how sad I am about Jean. I'm going to try to call you today, but I know you are just too overwhelmed to really absorb what is happening. I went to see Jean the day before she died. And I just stood and cried. That was not Jean in that bed. Our Jean was vibrant, and demanding, and full of life. She touched my life, like no one else has. She made it possible for me to have my dream. She put excitement, and joy, and passion into my life. Yes, she was demanding, and expected the best from us, but what some people do not understand is, that's what made us great. I will miss her. If you need anything, please let me know. You are both special people in my life. I say you are, because Jean will always be bigger than life to me.

Carol Kershner

My Tap Shoes on the Floor by Jill Fuller

I have a lot to be thankful for--- family, friends, health, and more'

But today I am especially thankful for—my costumes in the closet and tap shoes on the floor.

Over the past few years I have learned to dance--- to tap my life away.

It's been fun--- hard work--- and practicing practicing day by day.

Not many mistakes go by under Jean's eagle eye--- and I have learned to:

Point my toes; Keep in step; Smile, smile, smile!!!; Hold up my head; Precision; Teamwork; Smile, smile, smile!!!; Energy, energy; Keep in line; And all the while smile, smile, smile!!!

There are times when I thought I should pack it in,

Thought I'd never get it right--- even though I tried with all my might.

So now I'm a Hot Flash--- proud as can be.

When I dance on that stage I feel young and free.

The feeling I get when the show is over and the audience applauds, a standing ovation,

It's worth all the effort--- it keeps me at it---

And I'm glad I dance with the Hot Flashes.

Thank you Bernie, Marianne, and Kay

And to all my friends who have listened and helped along the way.

You see I have a lot to be thankful for--- But most especially,

My costumes in the closet and my tap shoes on the floor.

Remembering 1999 by Jill Fuller

Well another year has passed, and we are all together again – let's take a few minutes today and try to remember when:

Remember when the lights went out and we had to change clothes in the dark?

Remember when you had a heck of a time trying to find a place to park?

Remember when the music stopped, and we carried on dancing, never missing a beat?

Remember when we changed clothes in all that blasted heat?

Remember when Maxine decided to undress – while marching to St. Louis?

And Kay forgot Cerveza and acted like there was nothing to it?

Remember when some of us went the wrong way; our steps we forgot?

And a friend took your hand and led you to the right spot?

Remember when Jean was bitten by the cat?

And how Marianne keeps adjusting your hat?

Remember when Janice drove up in a bus?

Remember how Mary takes such good care of us?

Remember when Carol put on her show?

And Lynne swears she remembered to point her toe?

Remember when our steps got fancier and fancier?

And Marianne and Maxine heard the diagnosis of cancer?

Remember when Ricki colored her hair?

And someone almost fell off their chair?

Remember when Peggy's eyesight became worse?

Now Gloria drives her and helps her find her purse?

Remember how Maxine keeps asking for money?

When I'm in the poorhouse she won't think it's so funny.

Well, we have made it through another year – tap dancing side by side

Together we have lived, and laughed, and cried.

Our friendships have grown stronger throughout the past year,

Because we have shared our hope and our fears.

I wish you all good health in the New Year, and strength to carry through.

I'm so glad to be part of the Hot Flashes,

And can be here with all of you!

So, let's get our act together,

Let's go have some fun,

Let's dance side by side into the new Millennium!

I Decline to be Old! By Bob Hammond

Show biz 'bout to get me down …

So many gigs around this town …

All these tunes to resurrect,

Intricate steps to get correct.

This poor ol' brain is in a whirl –

How could I've thought I'm still a girl?

The calendar says I'm over the hill ..

One thing for sure – I'm off the pill!

So why am I hoofing it week after week,

Tapping the energy source that I seek?

How do I justify all of this work

For less than the pay of a company clerk?

Maybe it's something down deep in my soul …

Something that tells me I've gotta be whole.

Pushing my spirit up out of this rut

Opening doors that used to be shut.

Taking hands of people like me,

Learning the ways of terp-sick-oh-ree …

Ain't it a wonderful thing to behold,

How a dancer can answer: "I decline to be old!"

Salute to Jean

"Your life will change," she said to me
Way back in 1993
"Can't be," said I, "at 59."
"Oh yes," she said,"you'll fall in line."

"The stage, I fear, is slick and rickety;
I don't intend to be persnickety."
"Oh me," said she, "for heaven's sakes,"
We Hot Flashes do whatever it takes."

"A commercial is just what we need," said Jean,
"A tap dancing video, is that what you mean?"
"Of course," said she, "I'll call today."
"Health Partners will tell us," 'We want you this day.'

"The big time came with our New York run,"
Said Jean, "Your dancing days are far from done."
"Thanks, Jean, to you and 'Favorite Son,"
"Columbus Circle, New York Times, a TV show, all were done."

"Guess what?" Said Jean, "you will say," 'Wow!'
"Senior Olympics wants us now."
"Jean, thousands in the crowd there'll be."
"We can do it; you will see."

"Let's enter some contests and strut our stuff."
"My goodness, Jean, that will be tough."
"No way," said she, "we'll show our mettle."
"In Vegas count on six gold medals."

"Trophies, trophies everywhere,"
Jean, "wherever we look not a shelf is bare."
"On the Telethon you took your chance."
Jean said, "I'm very proud of how you danced."

"From New York, Vegas, to Hollywood,"
"We did," Jean said, "the best we could."
Said I, "My life did change, I had my fling."
"Your praises I'll forever sing."

BY LEONA CLAIRE FULLER

The Hot Flashes

Made in the USA
Charleston, SC
08 October 2014